This NoteBook Belongs to:

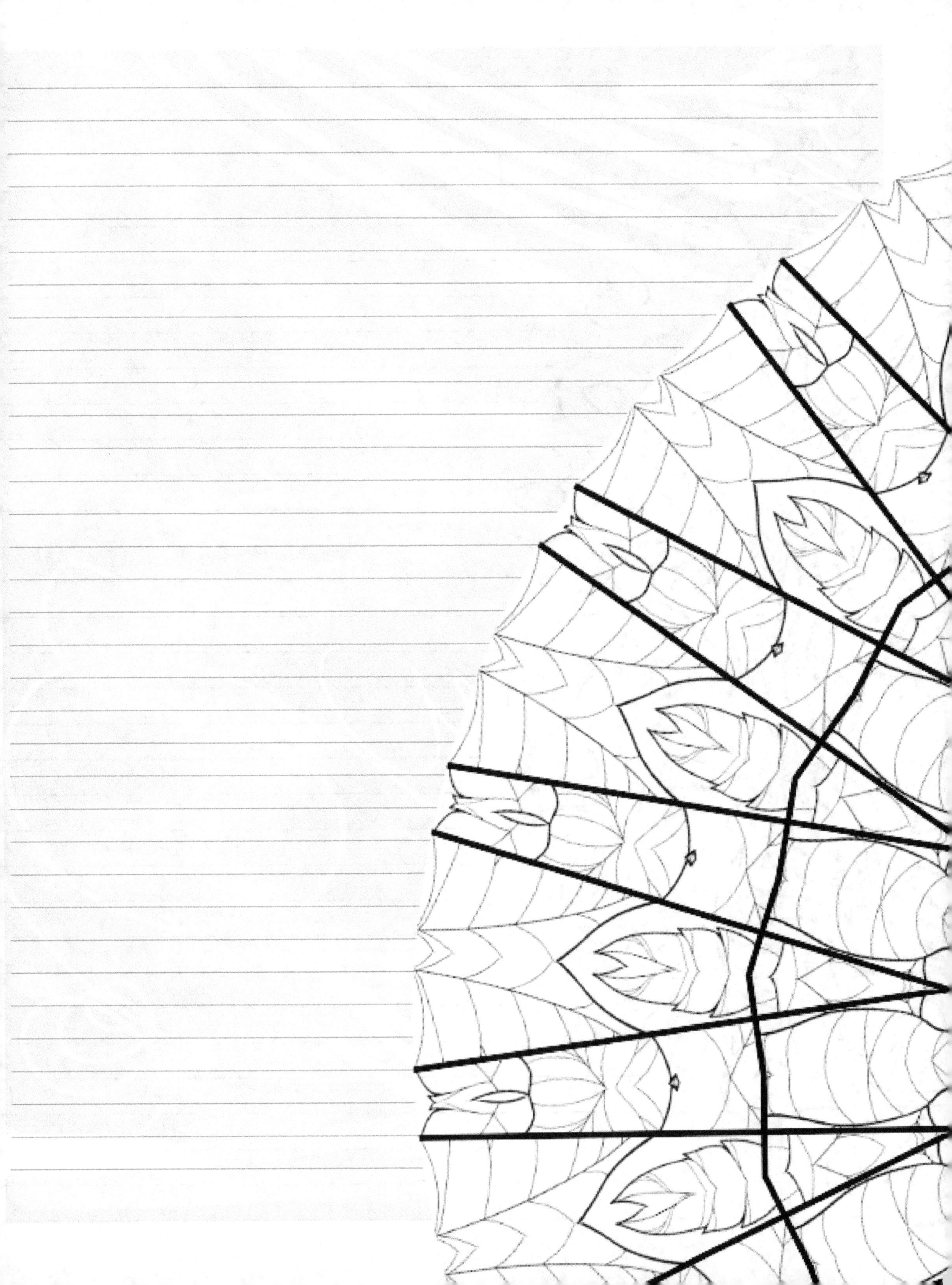

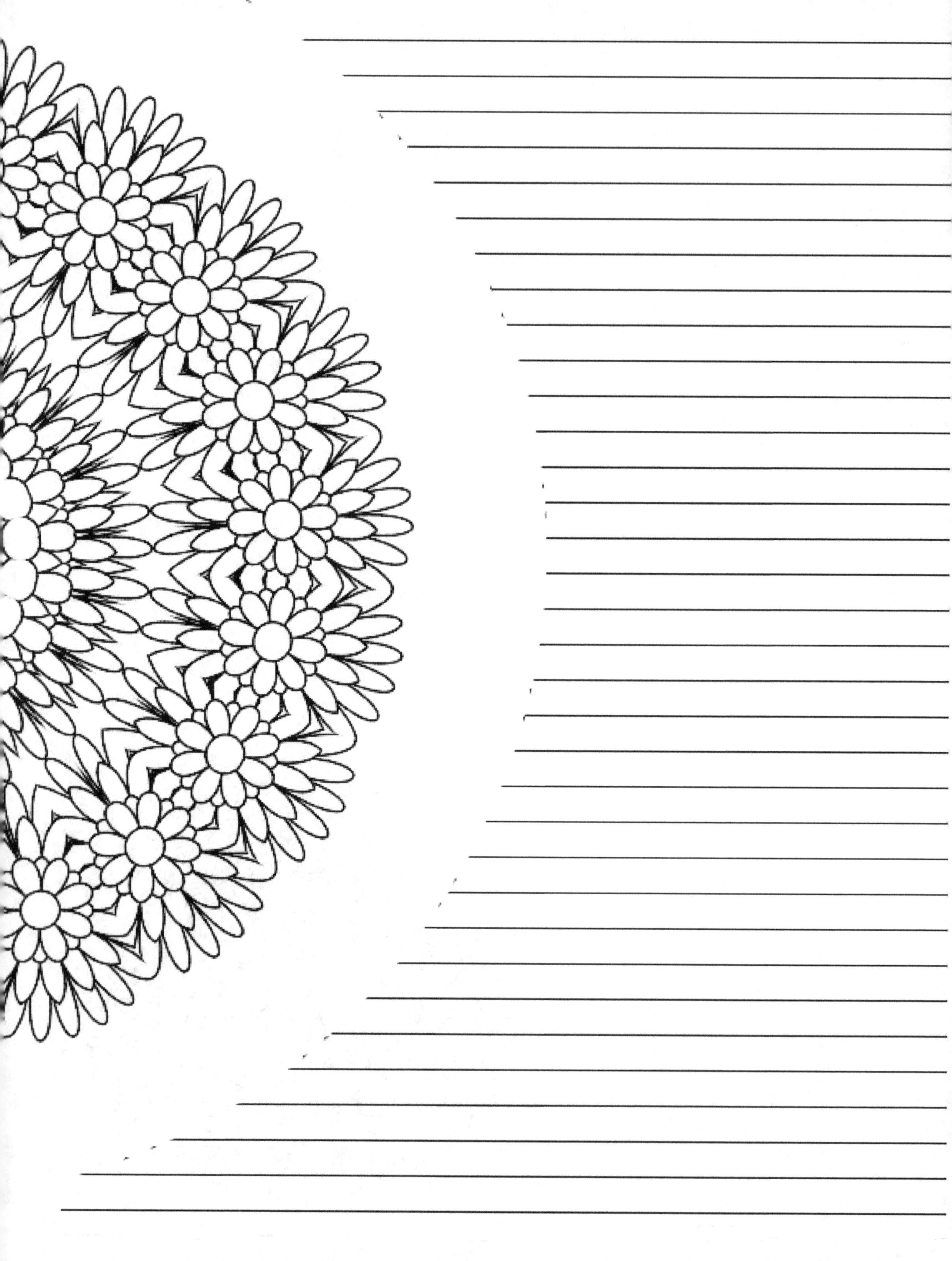

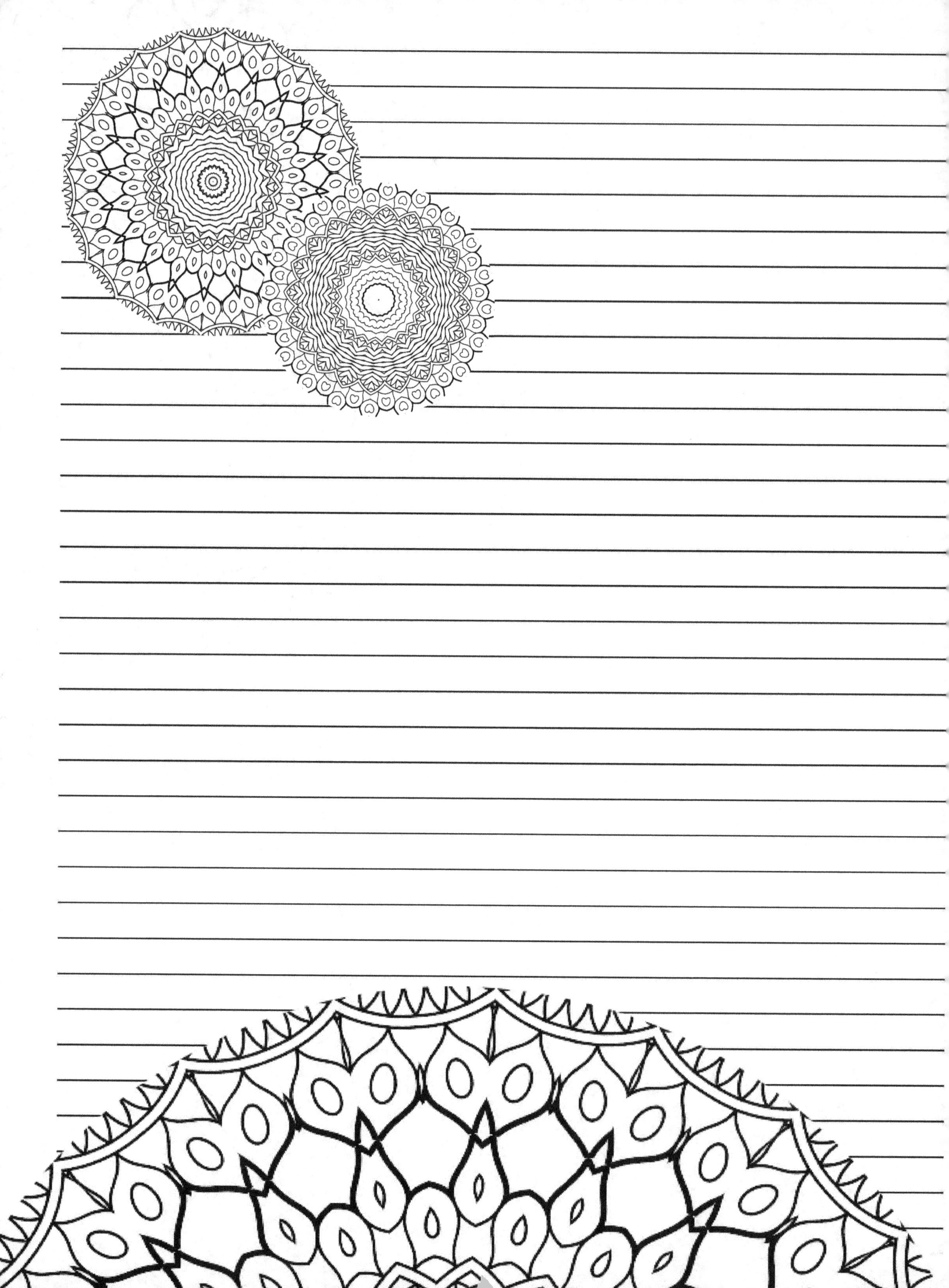

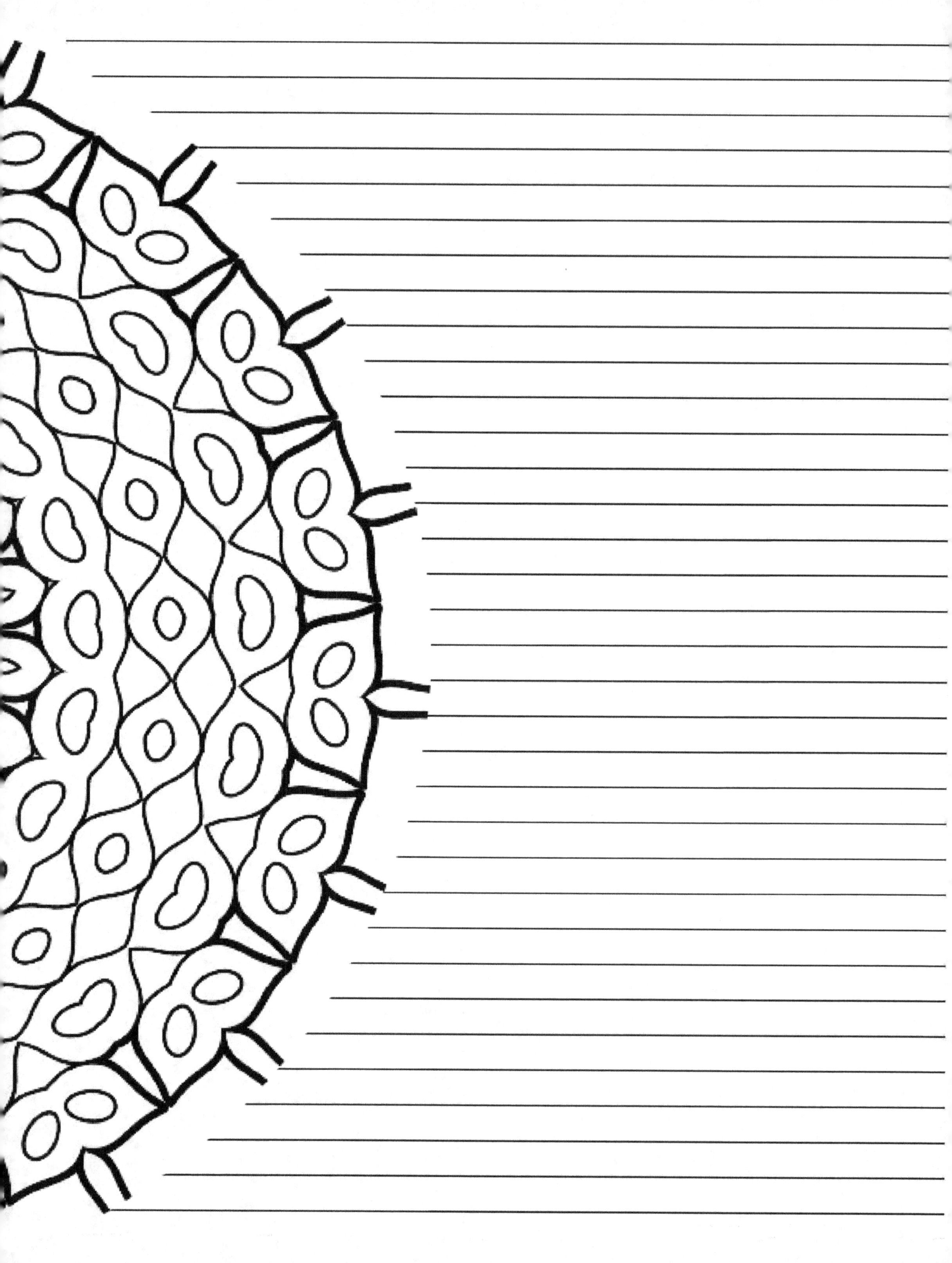

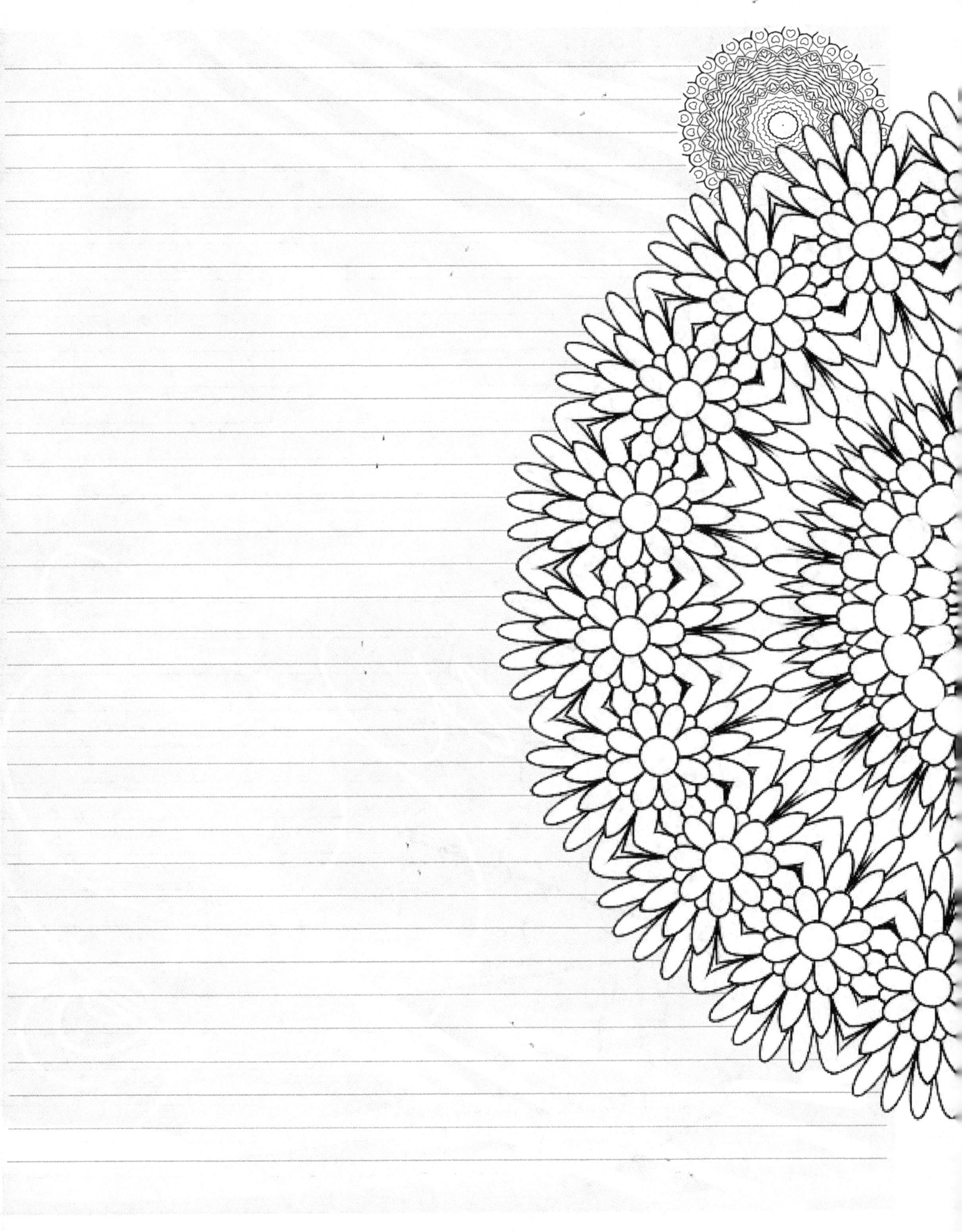

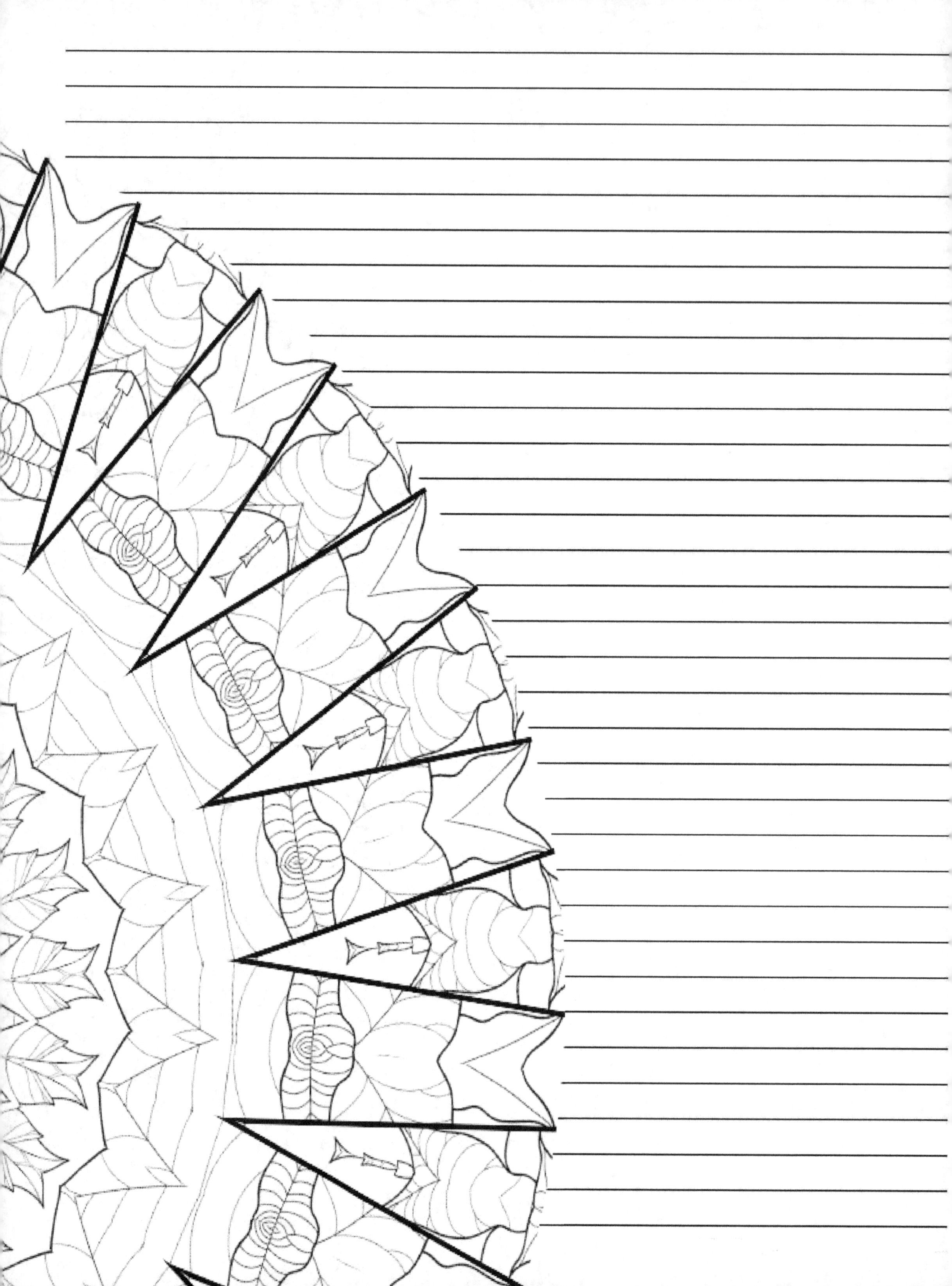

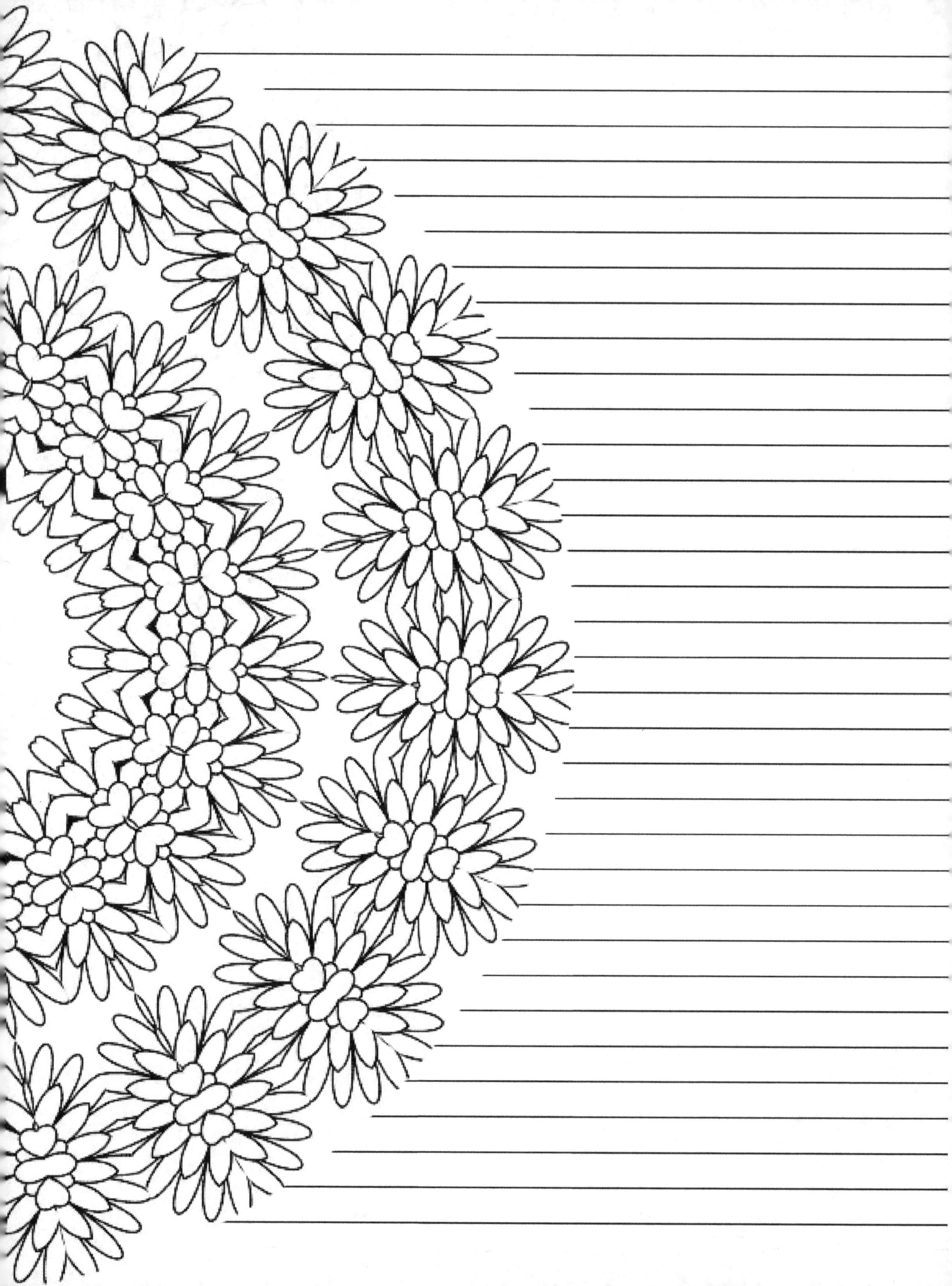

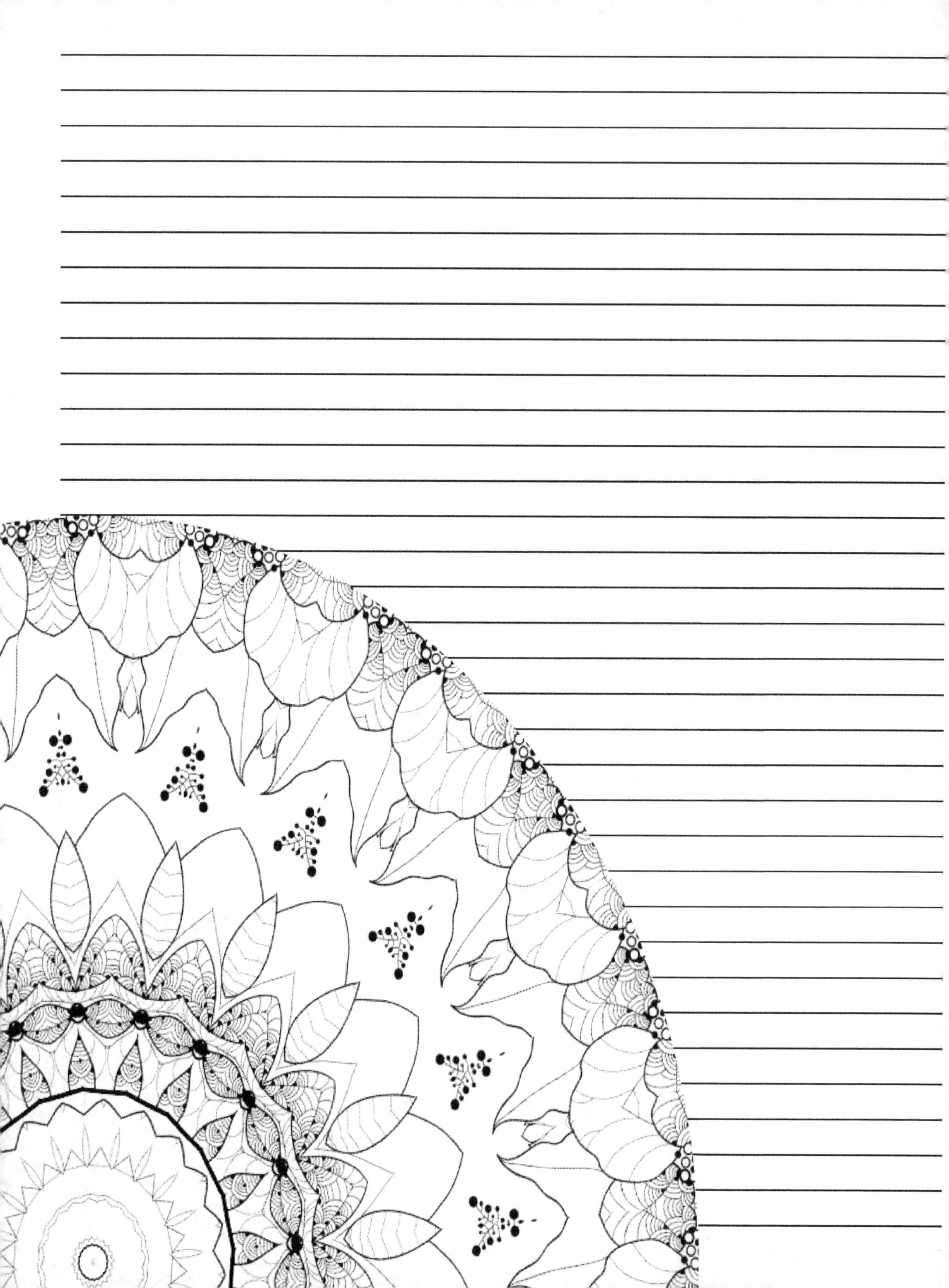

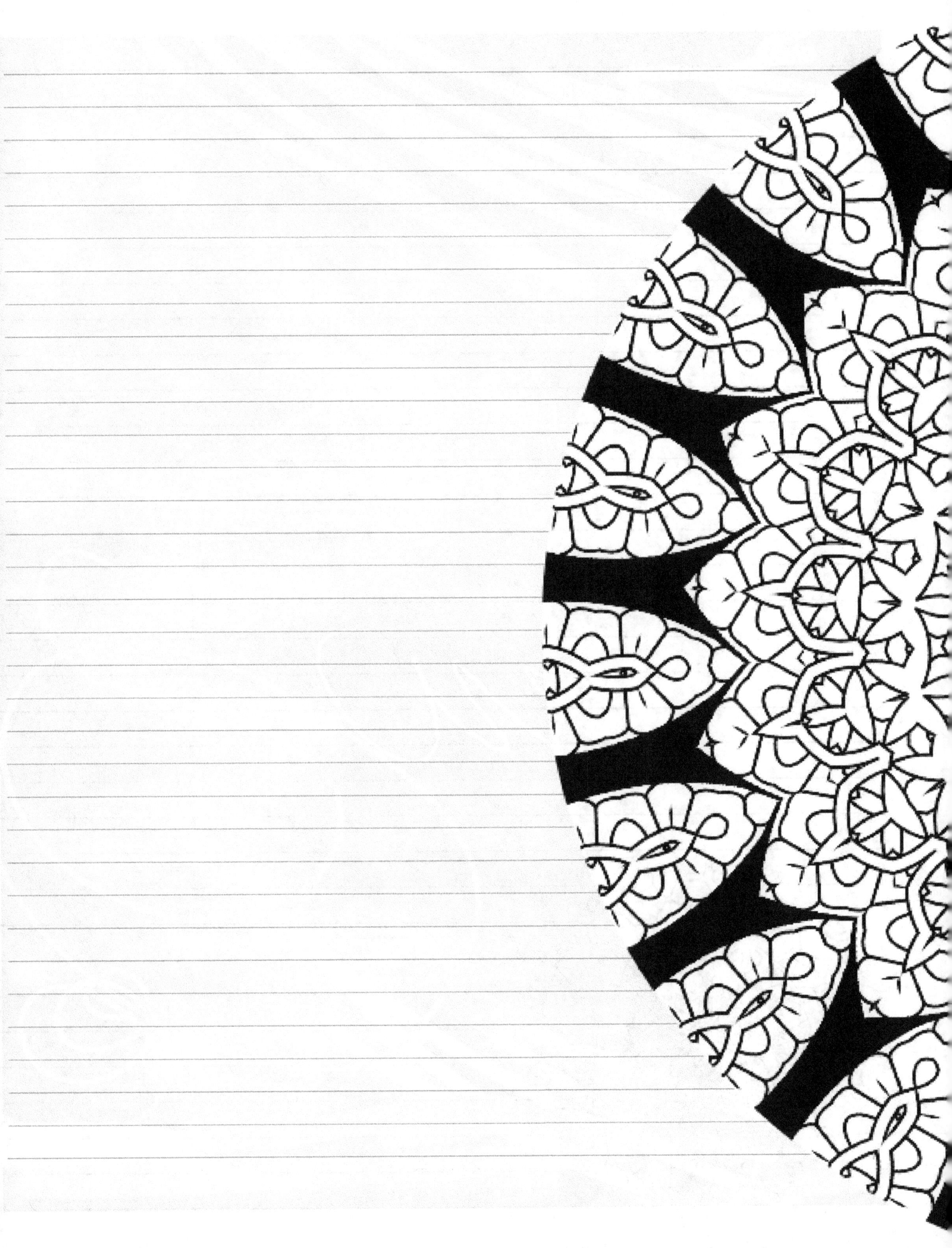

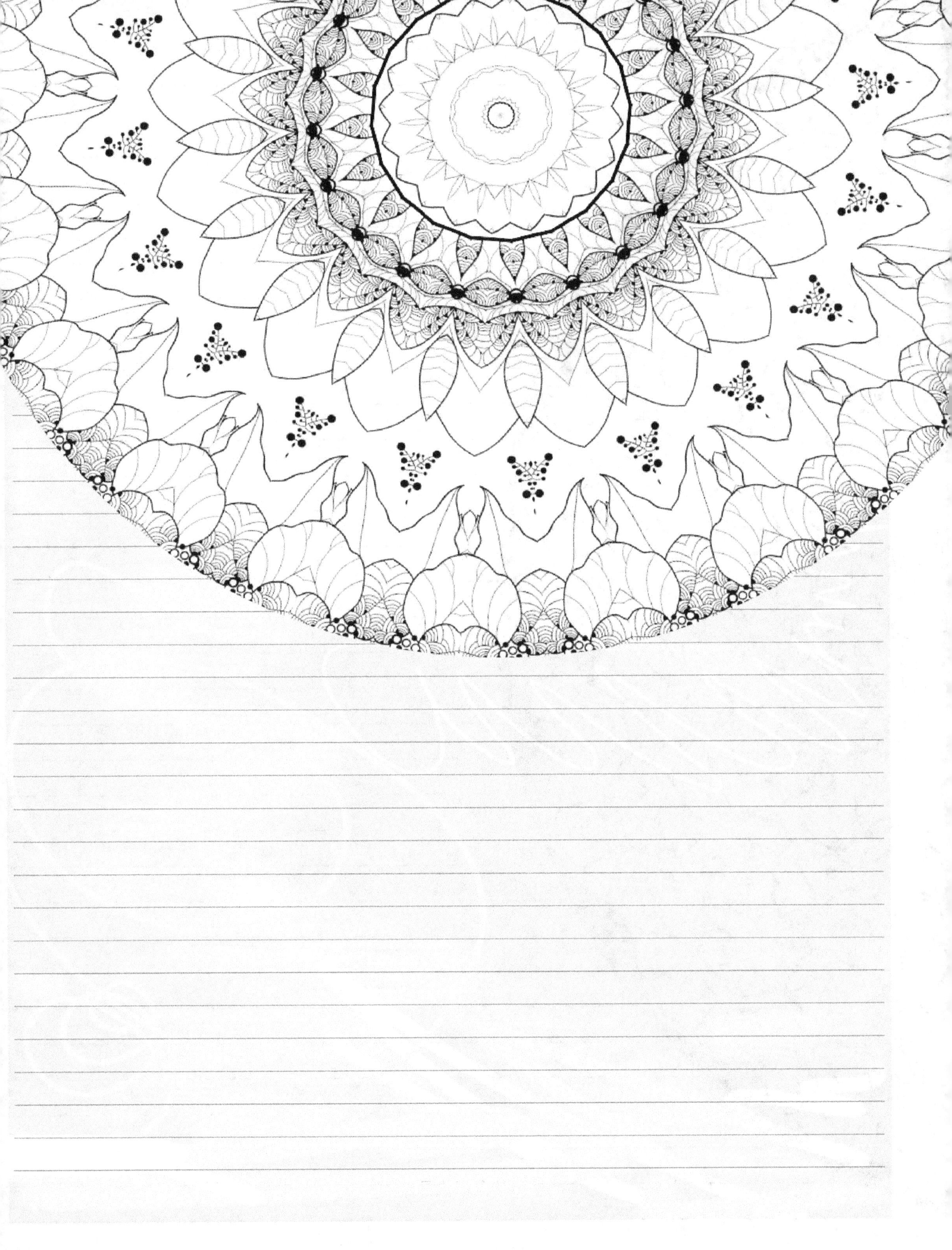

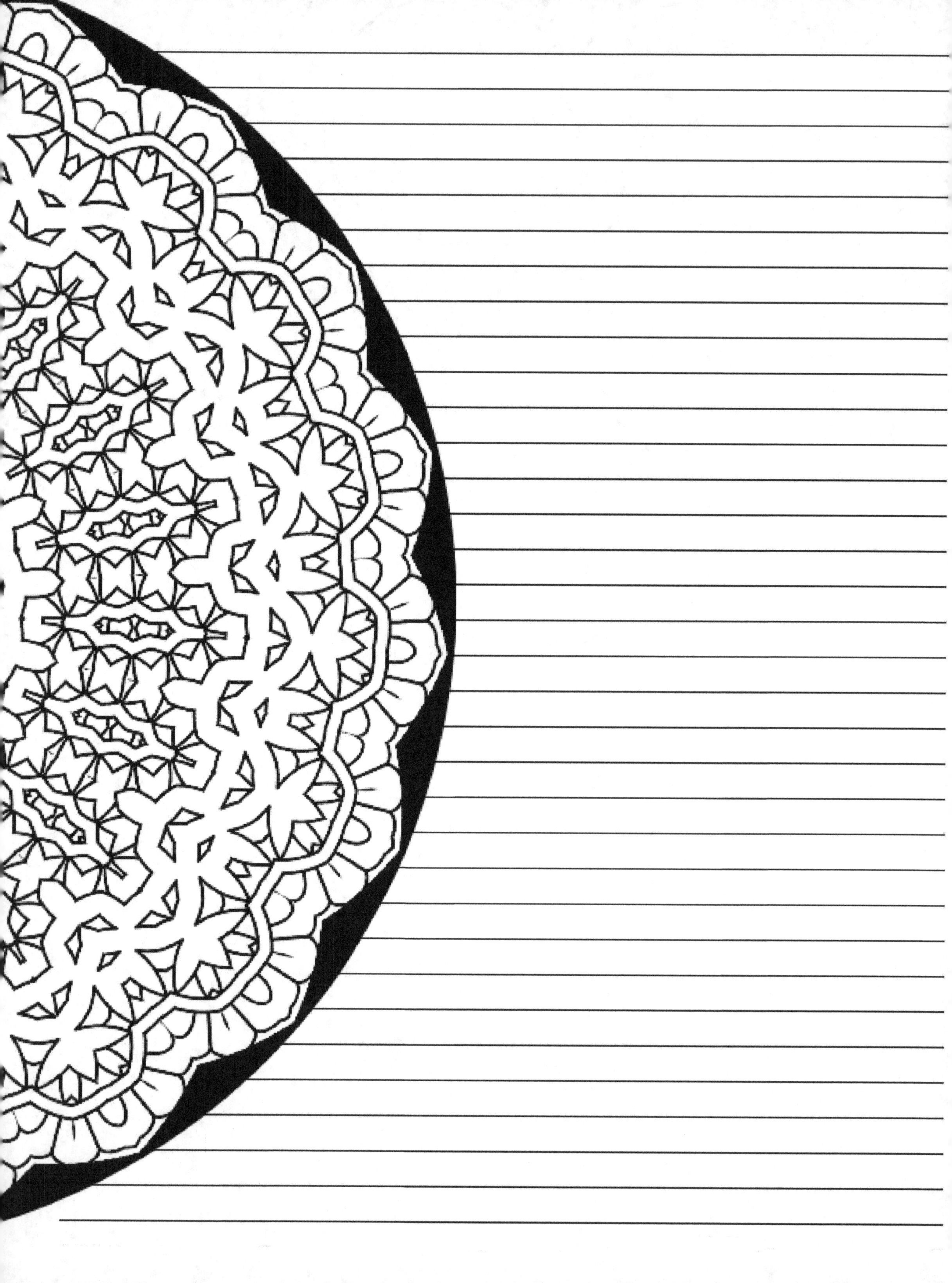

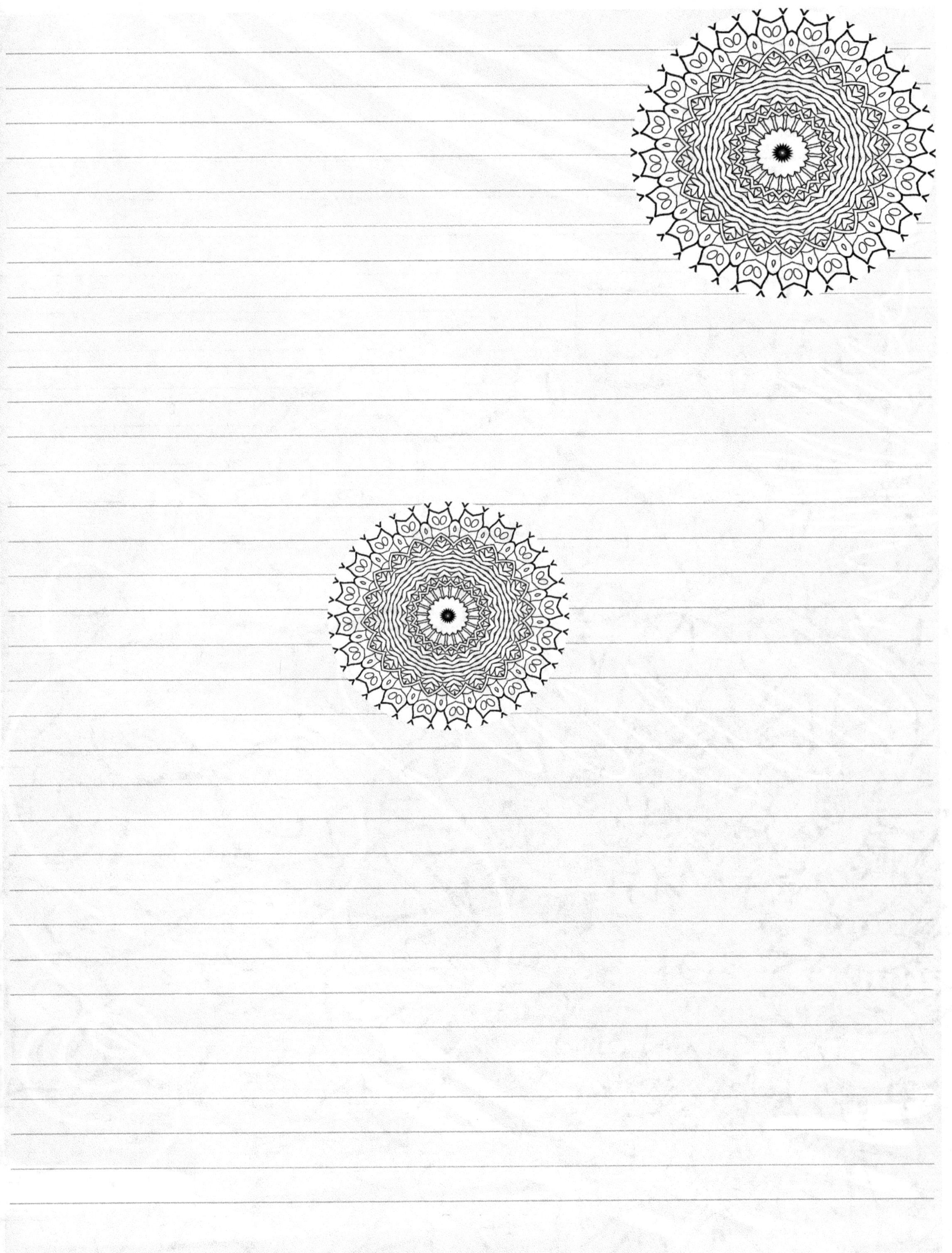

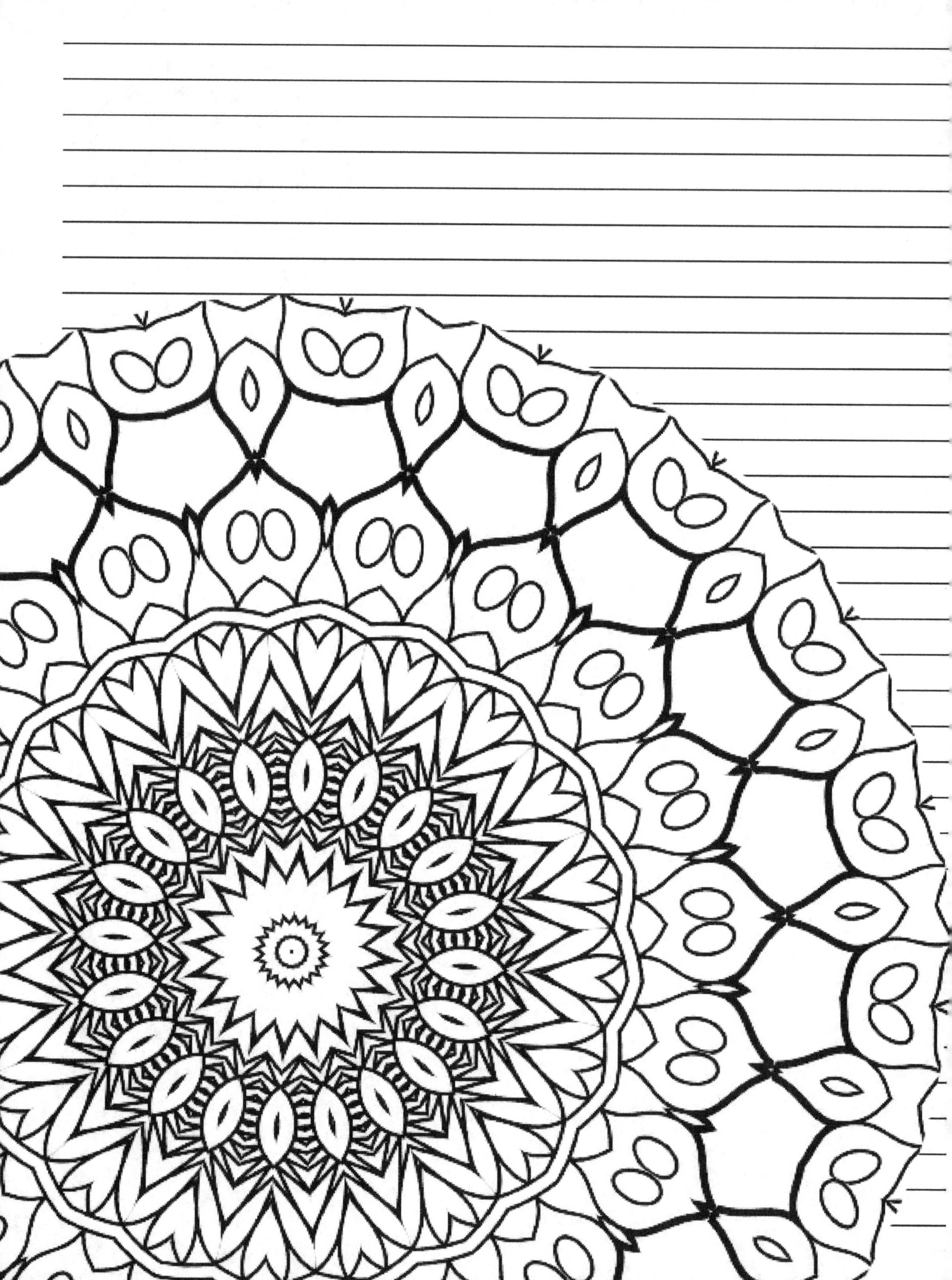

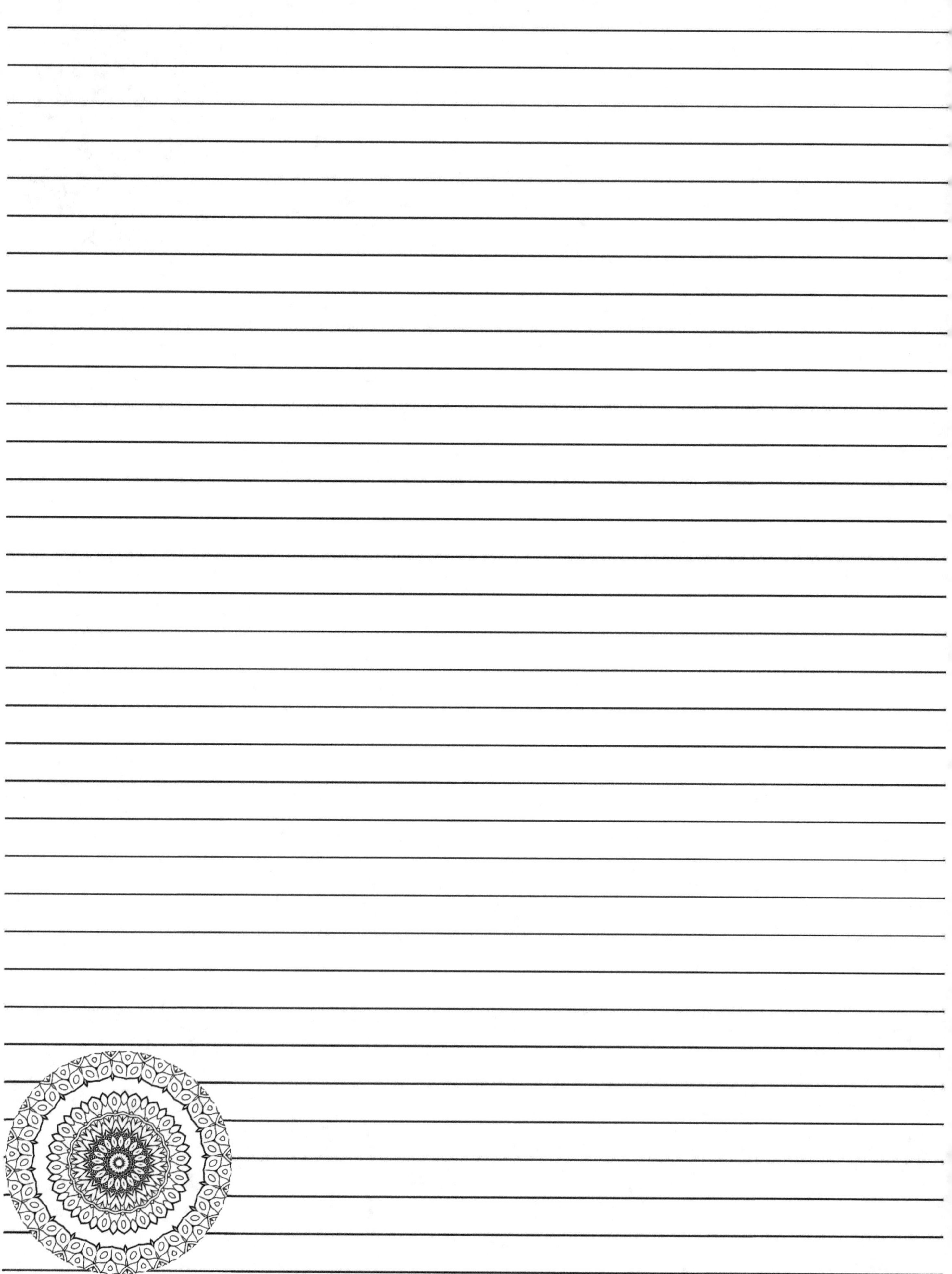

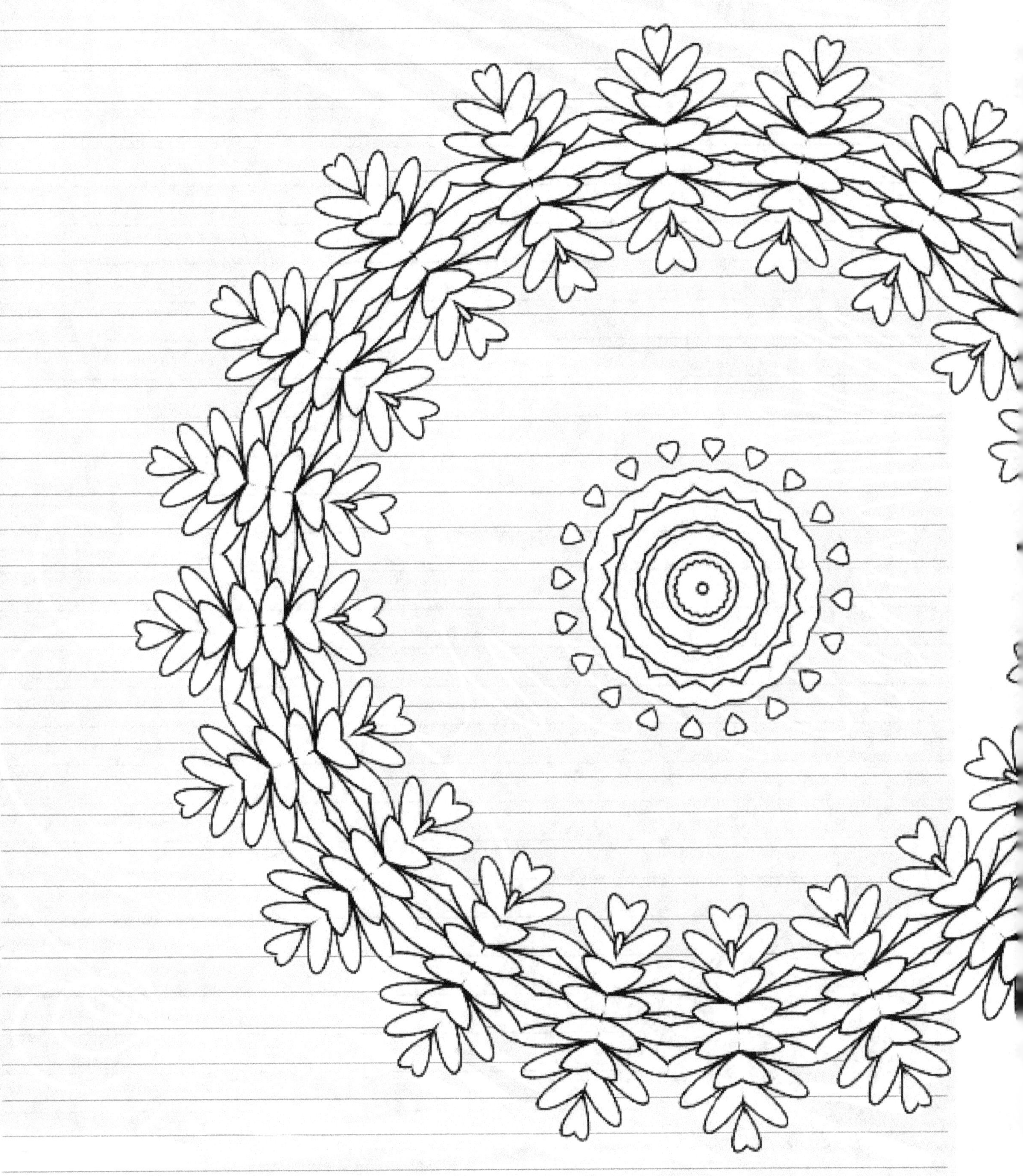

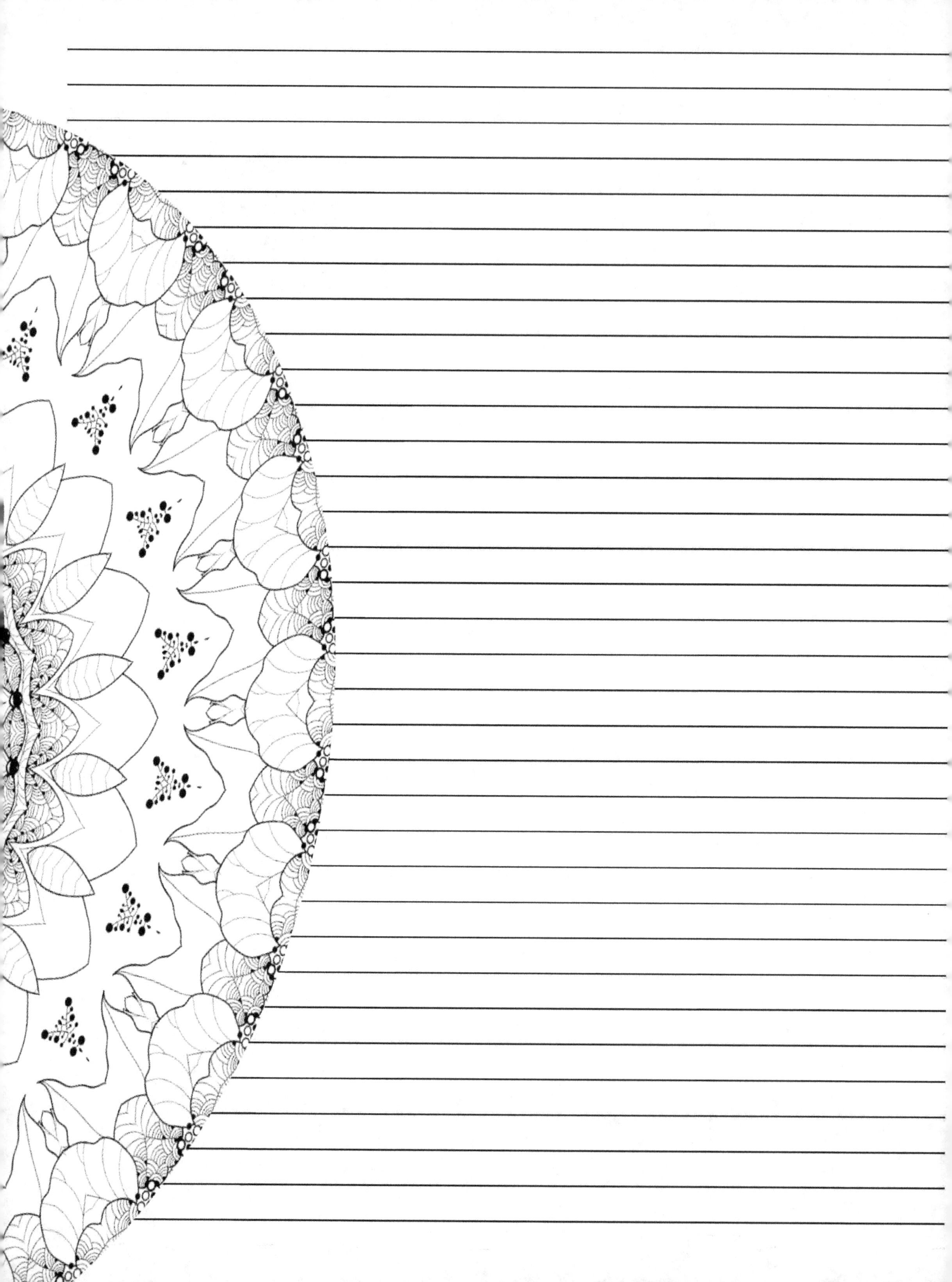

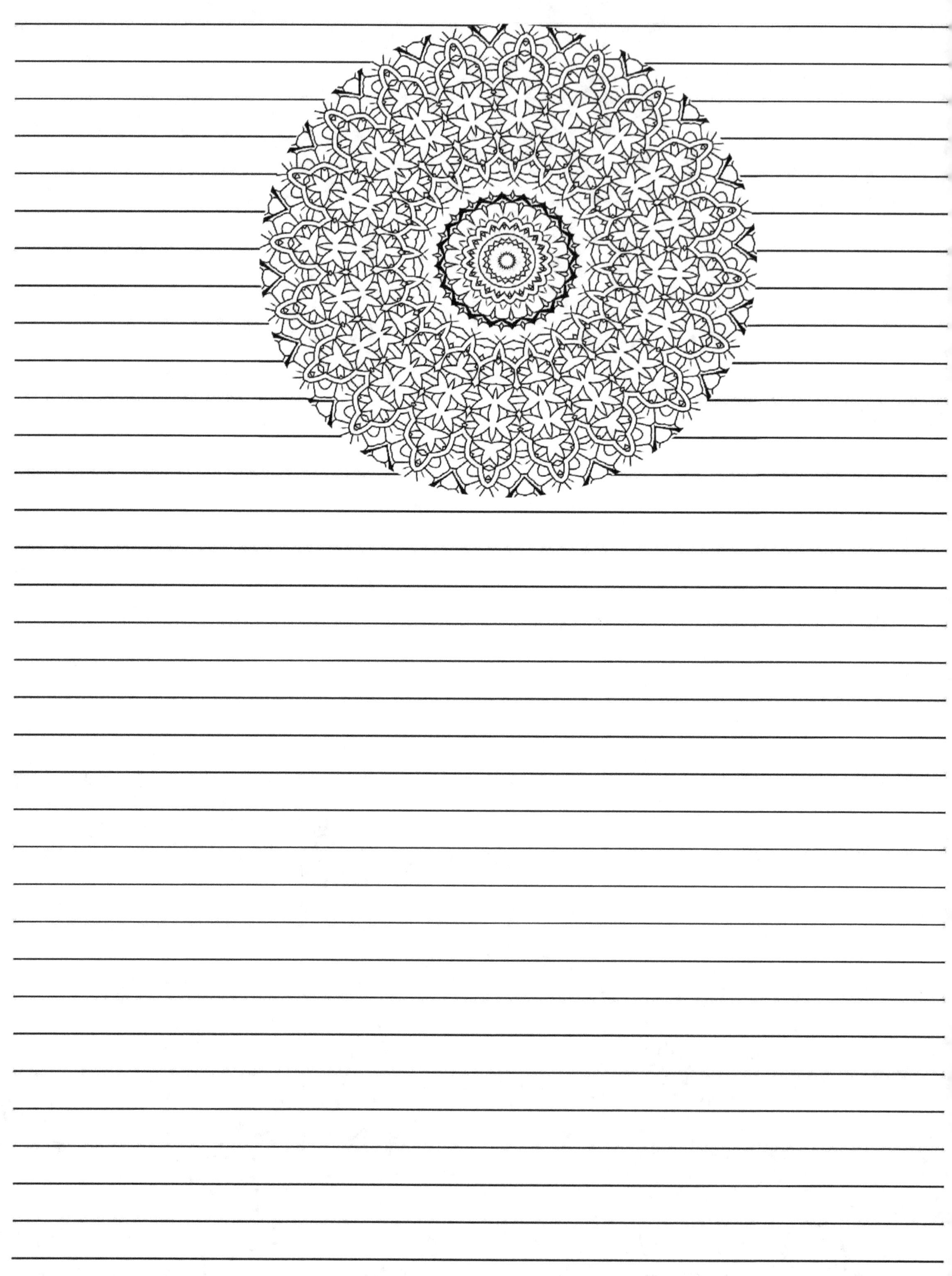

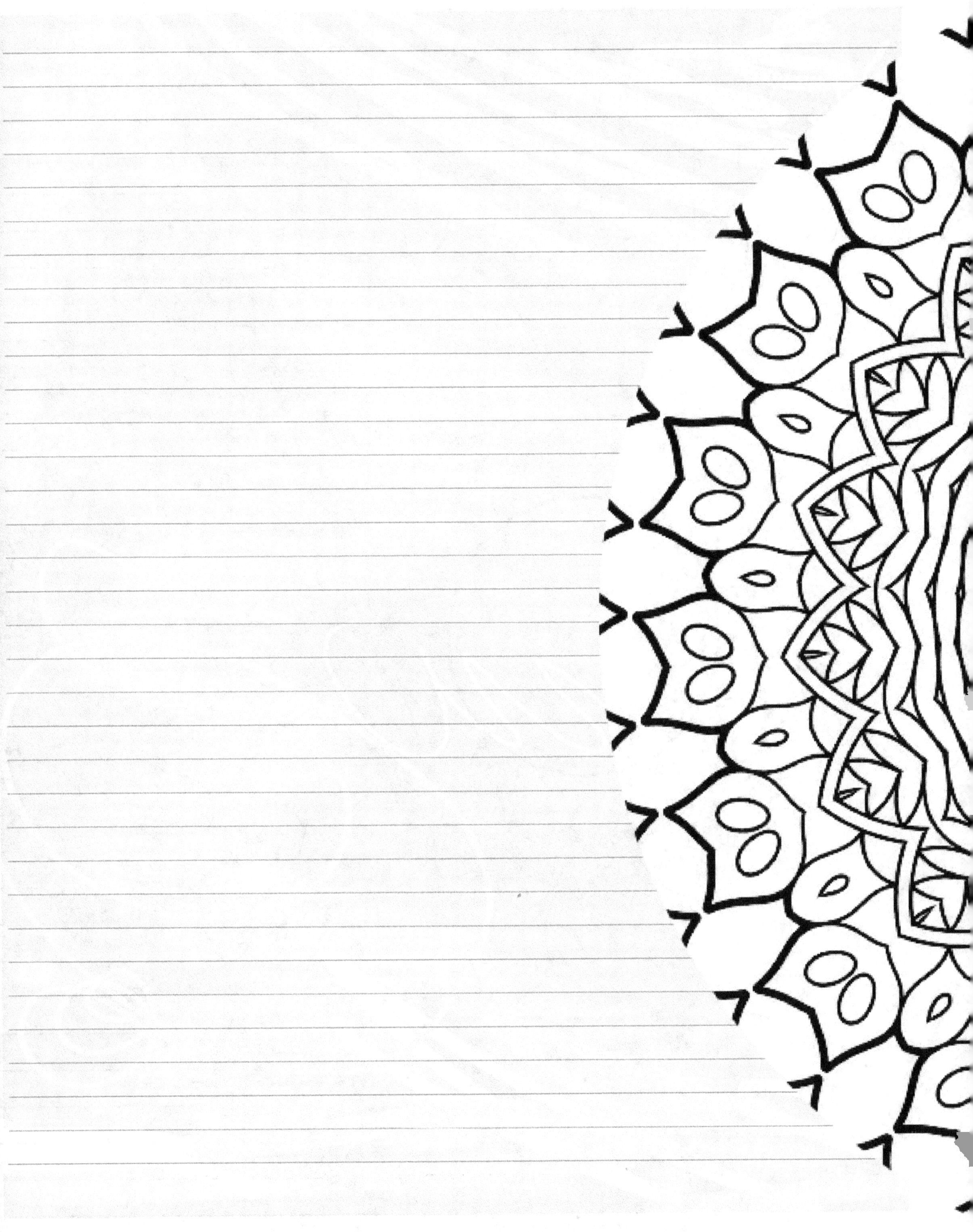

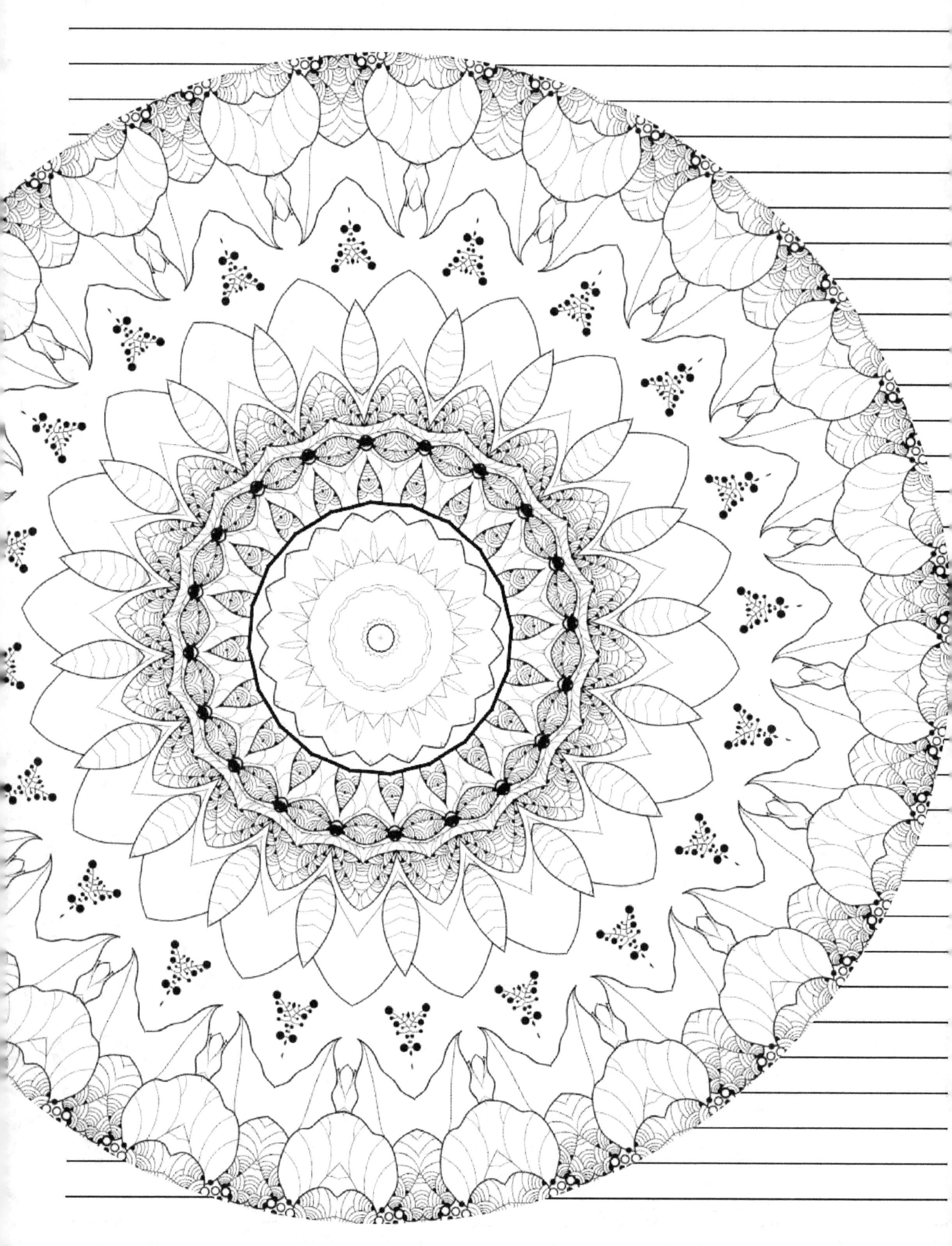

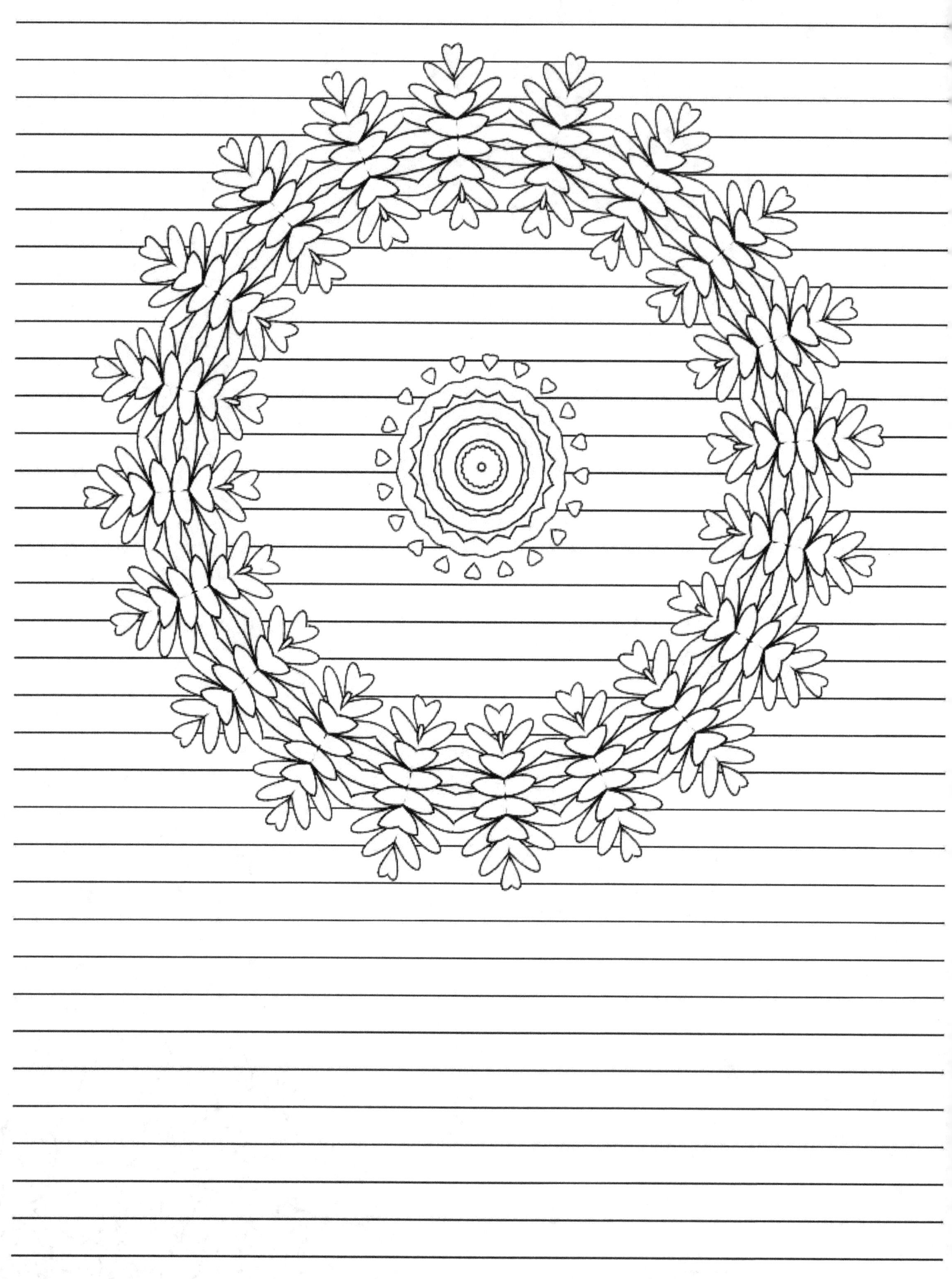

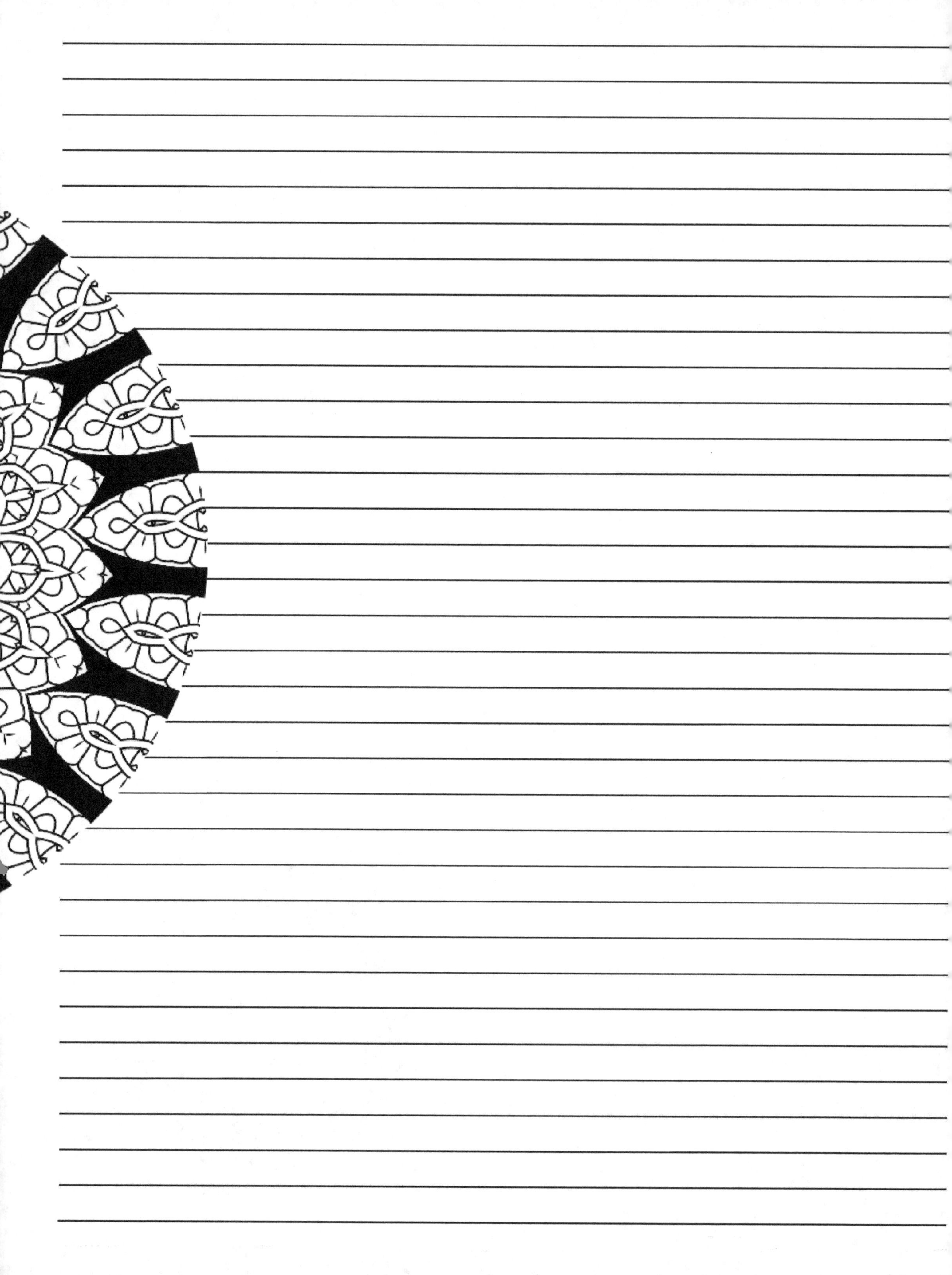

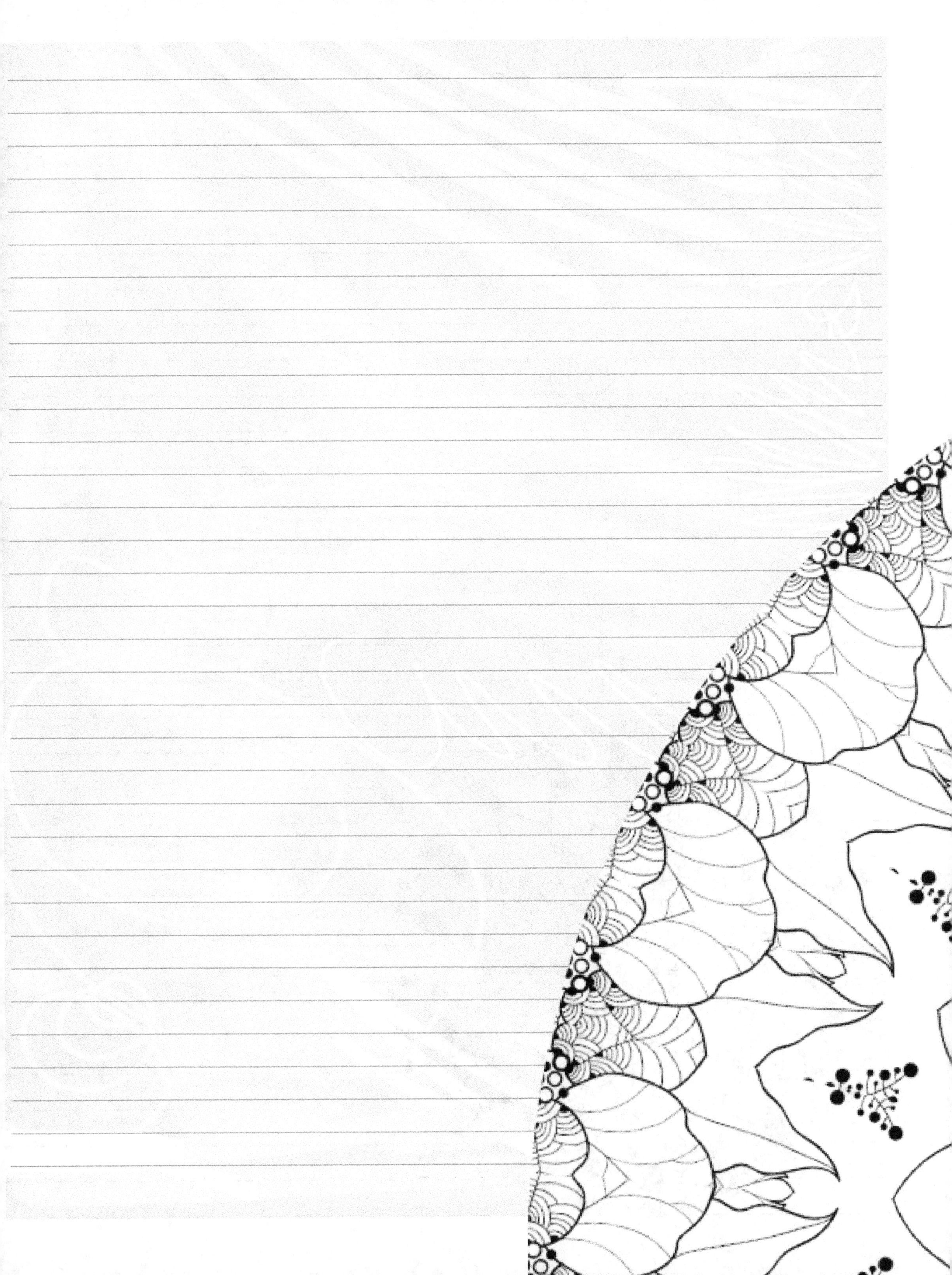

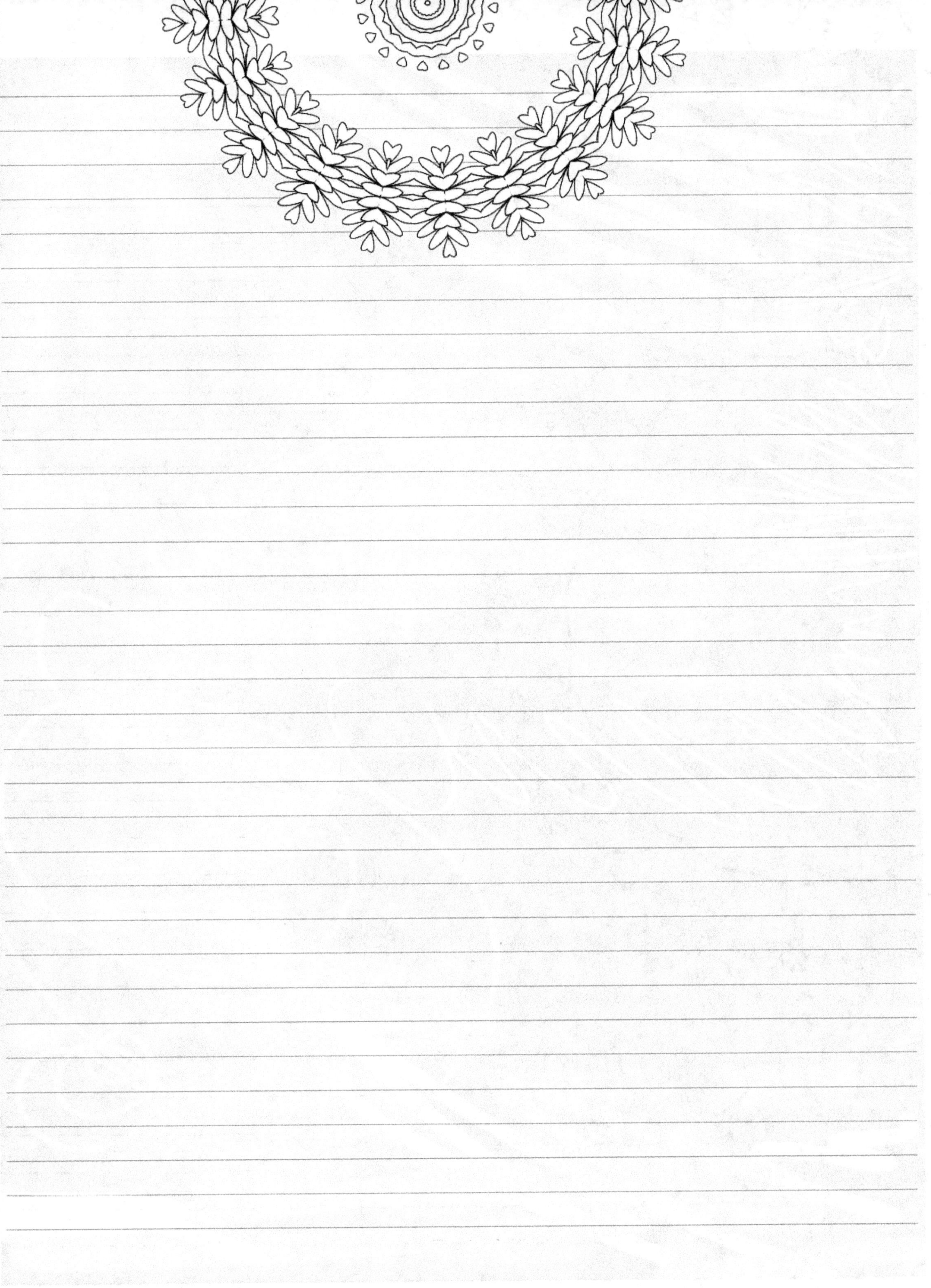

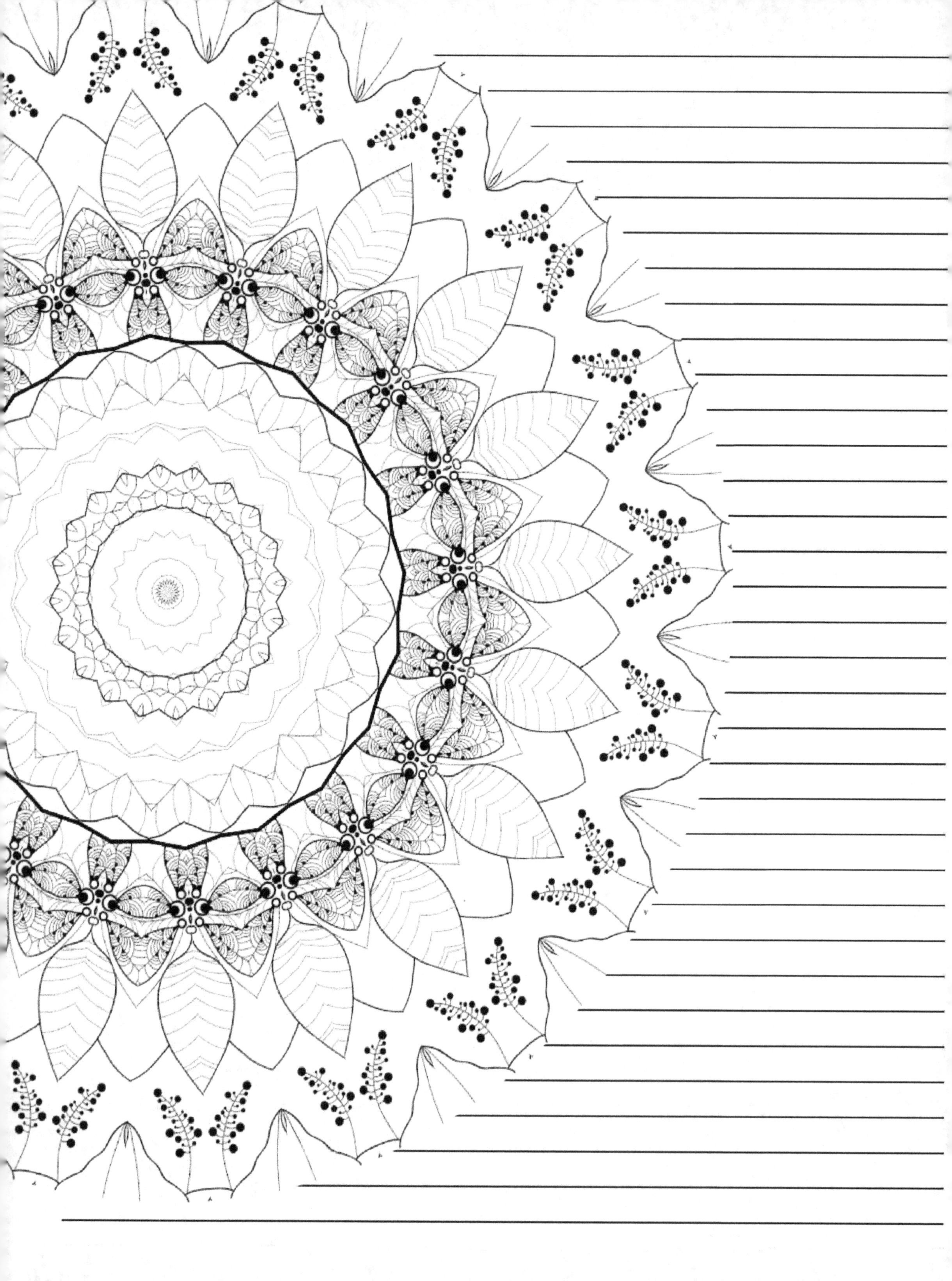

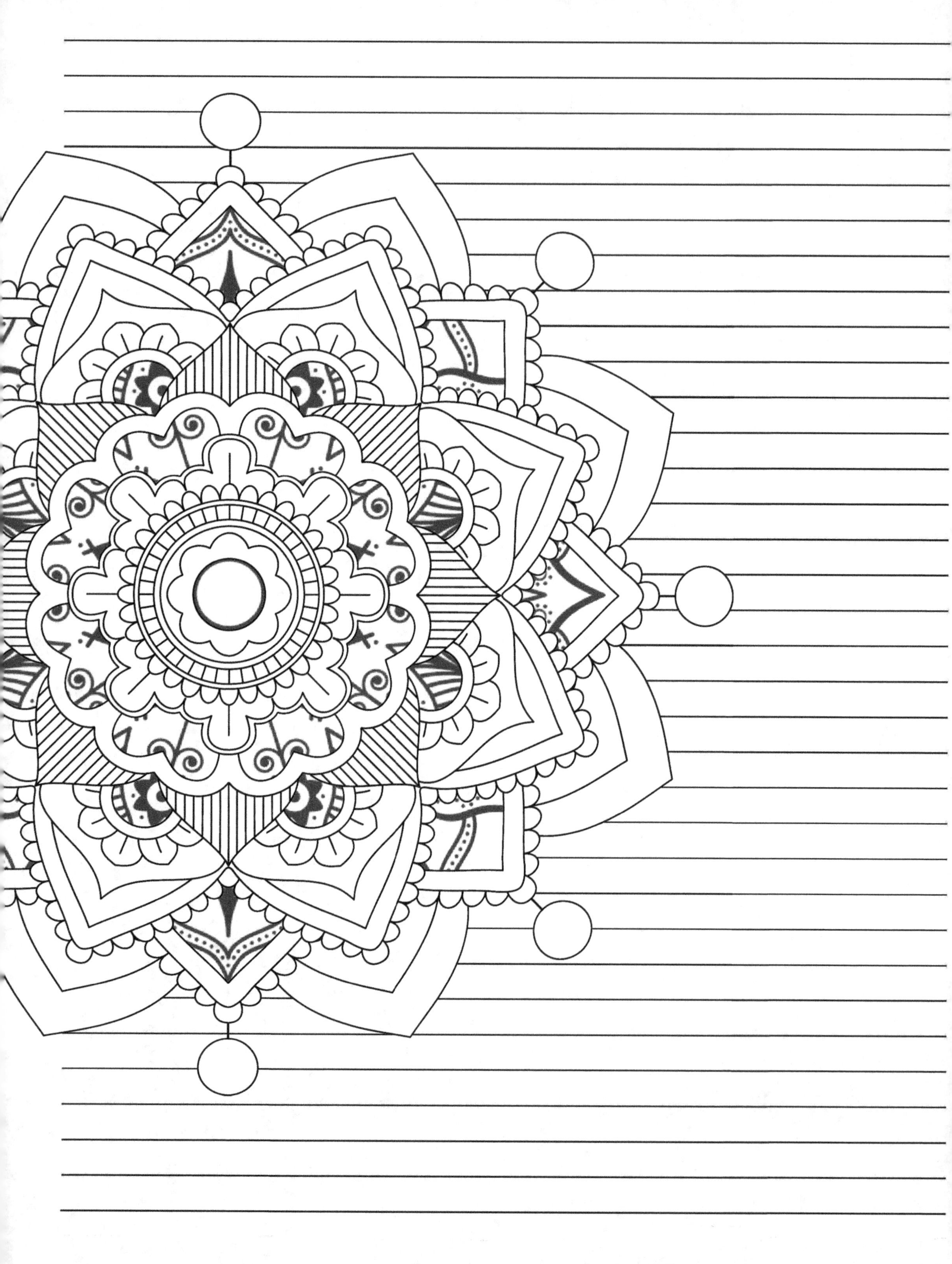

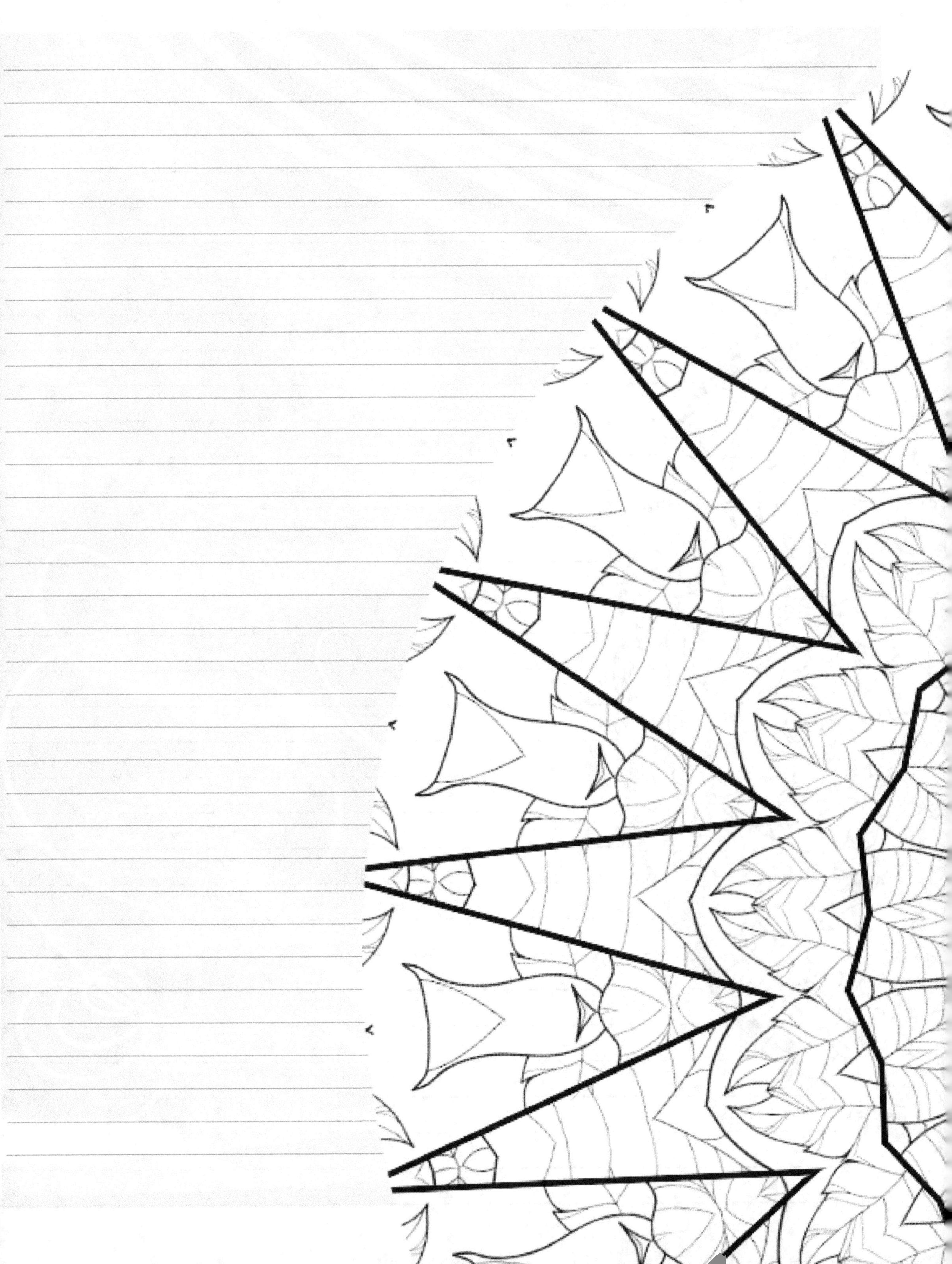

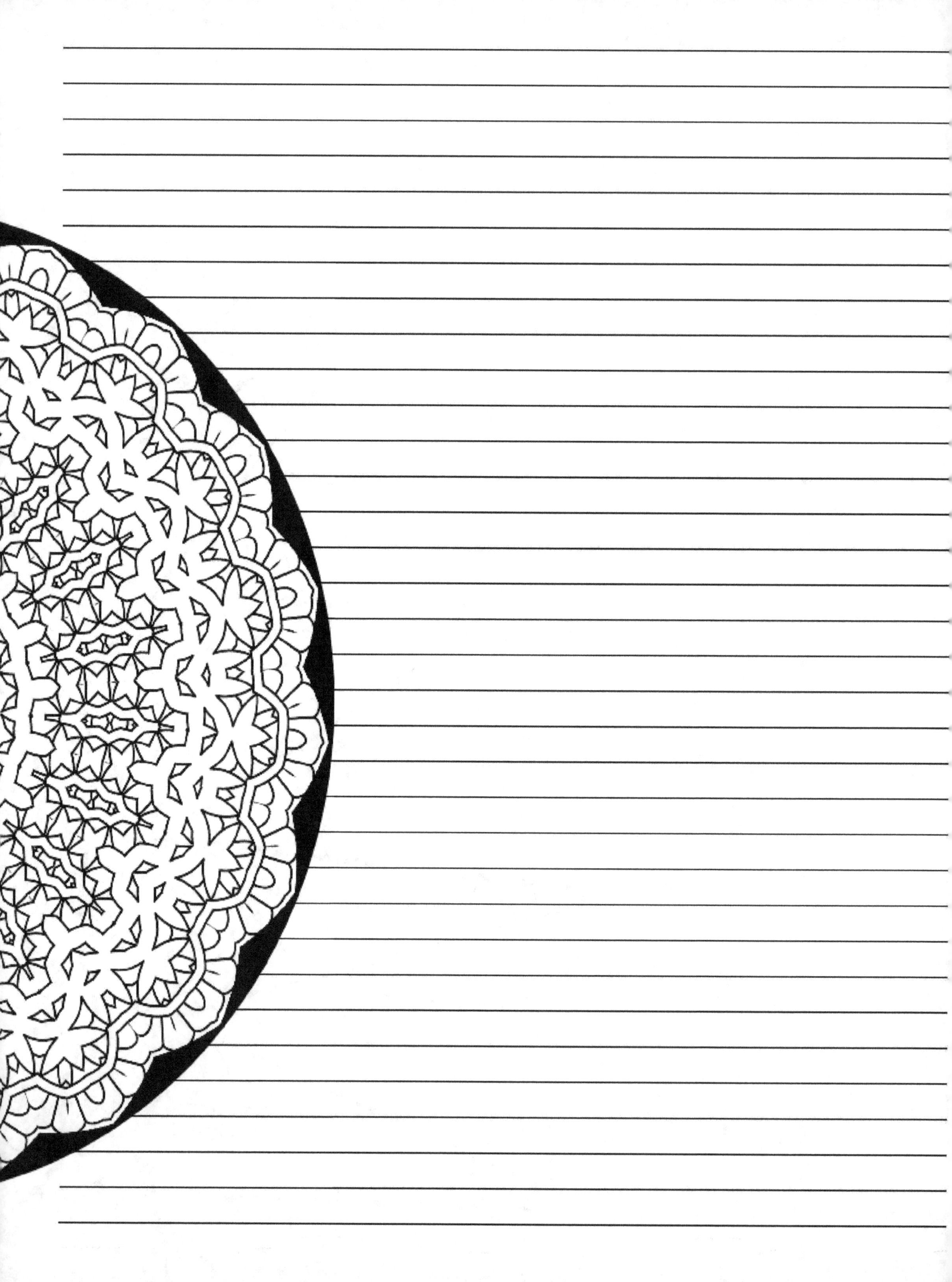

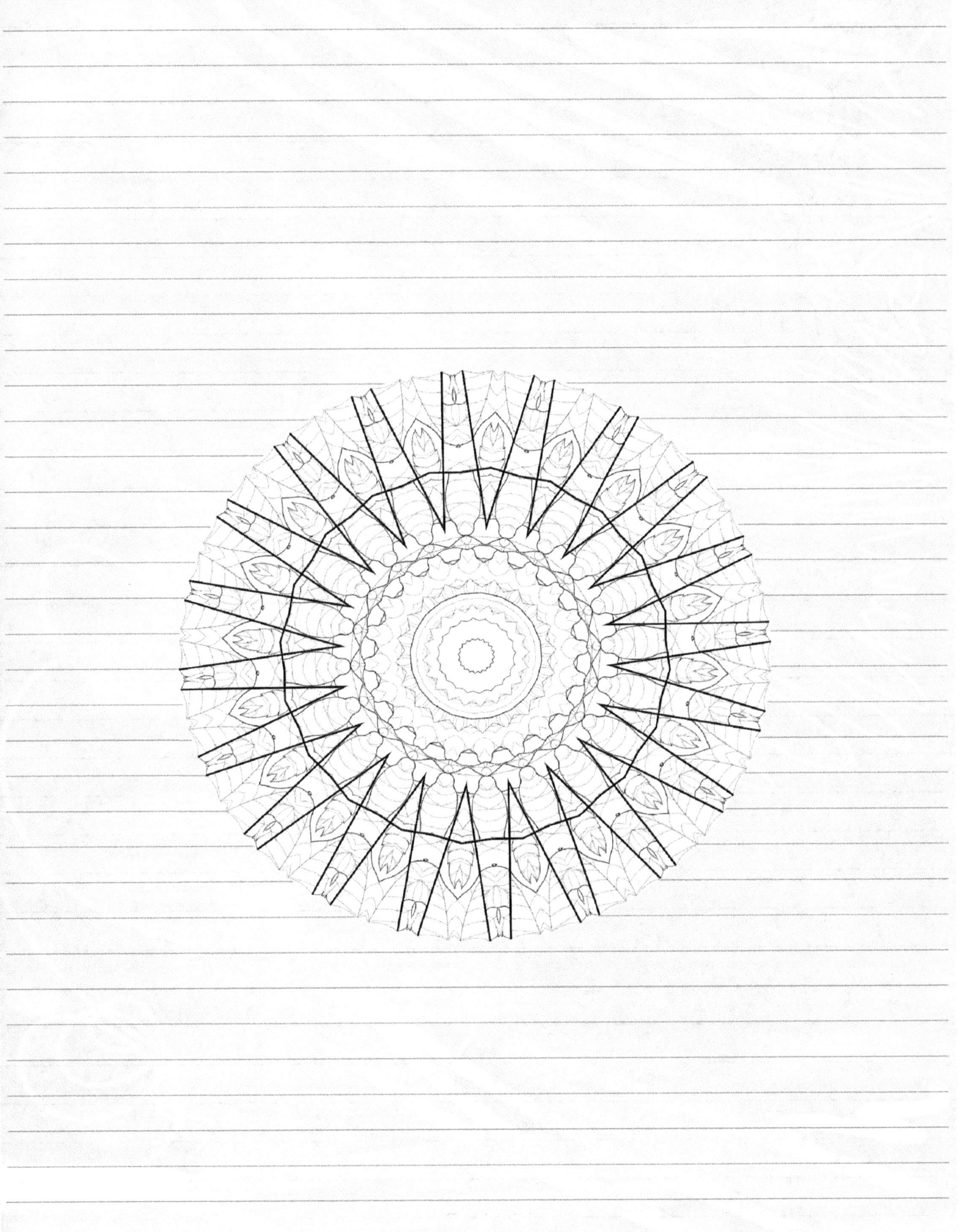

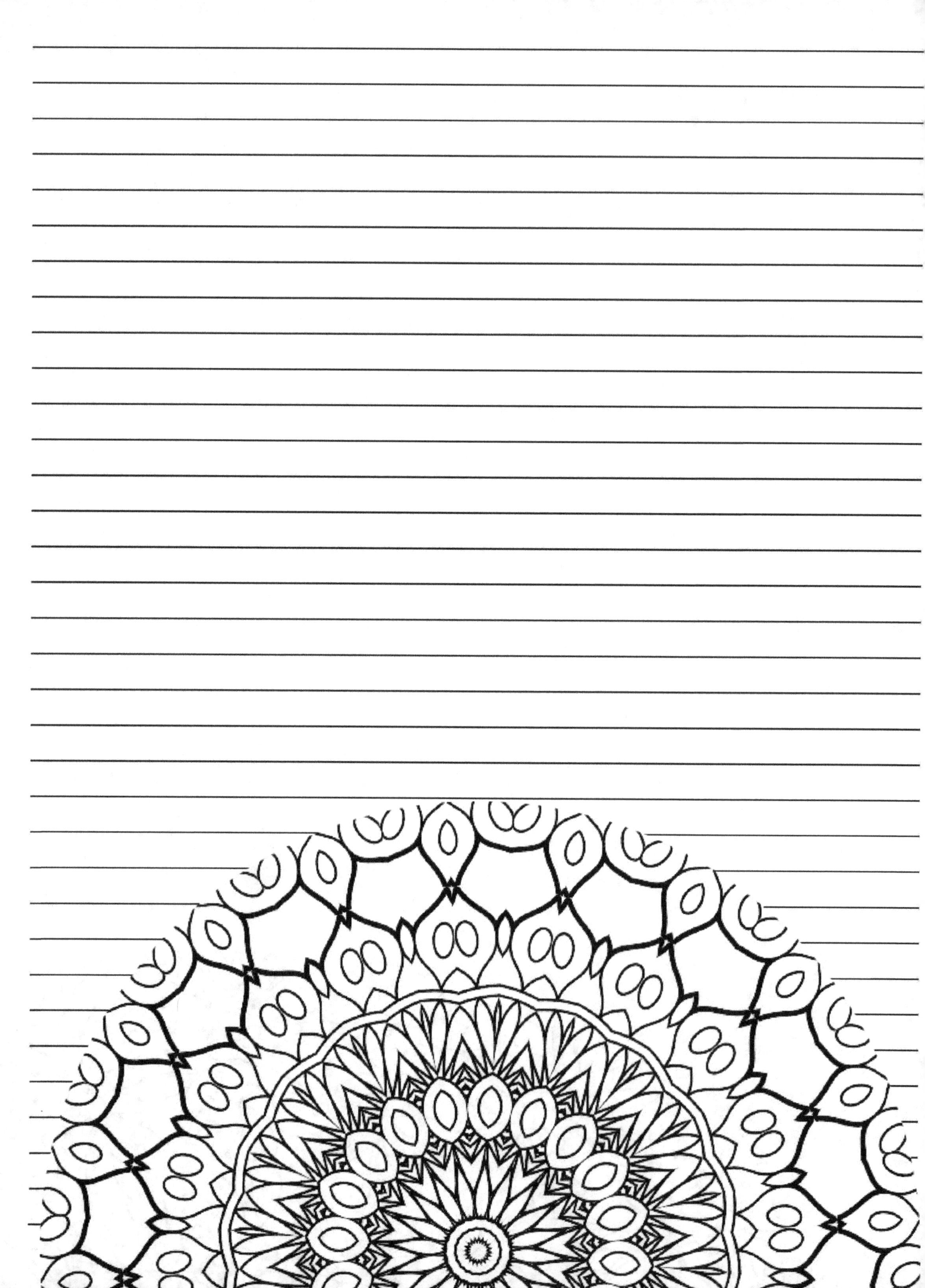

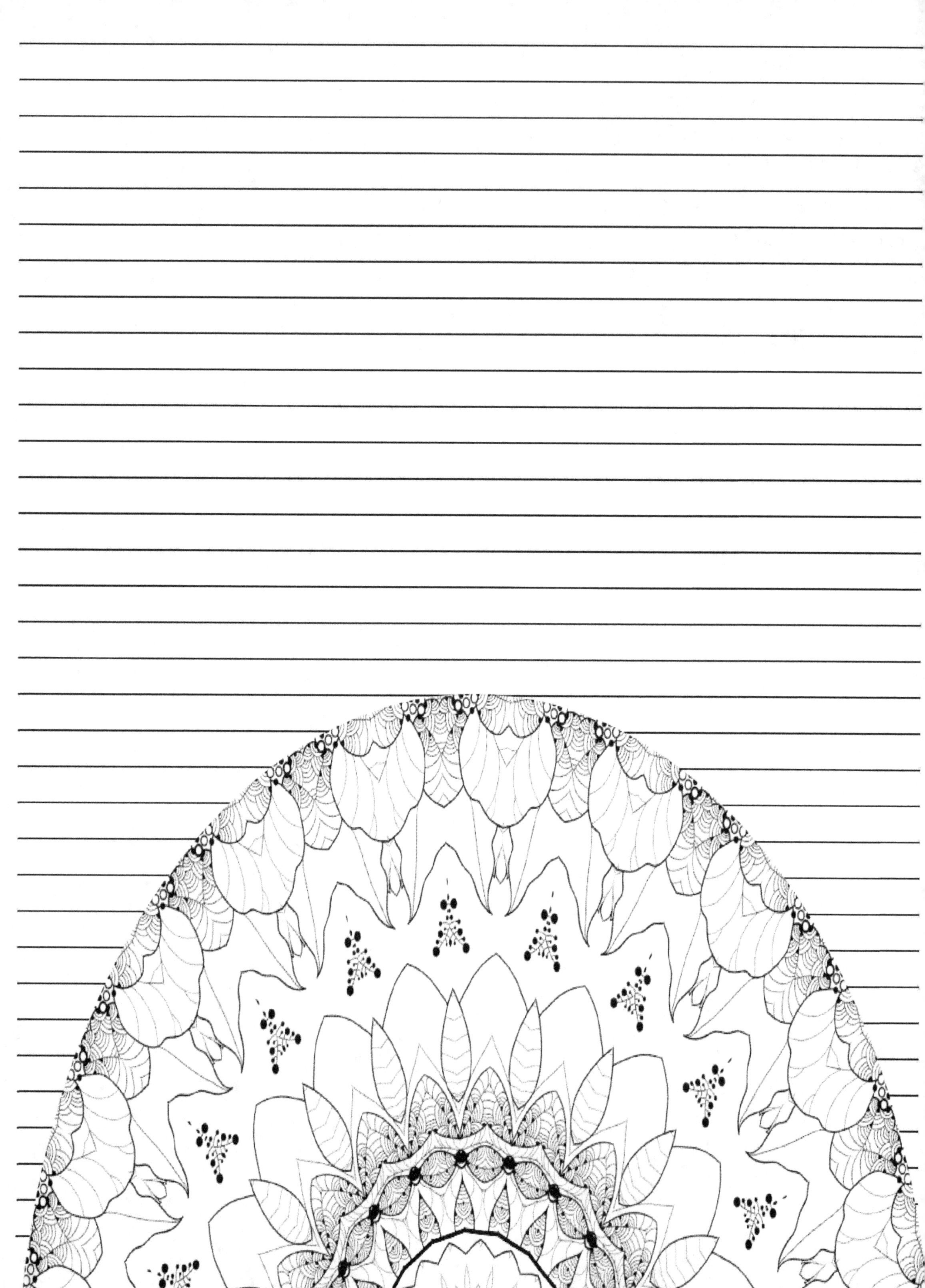

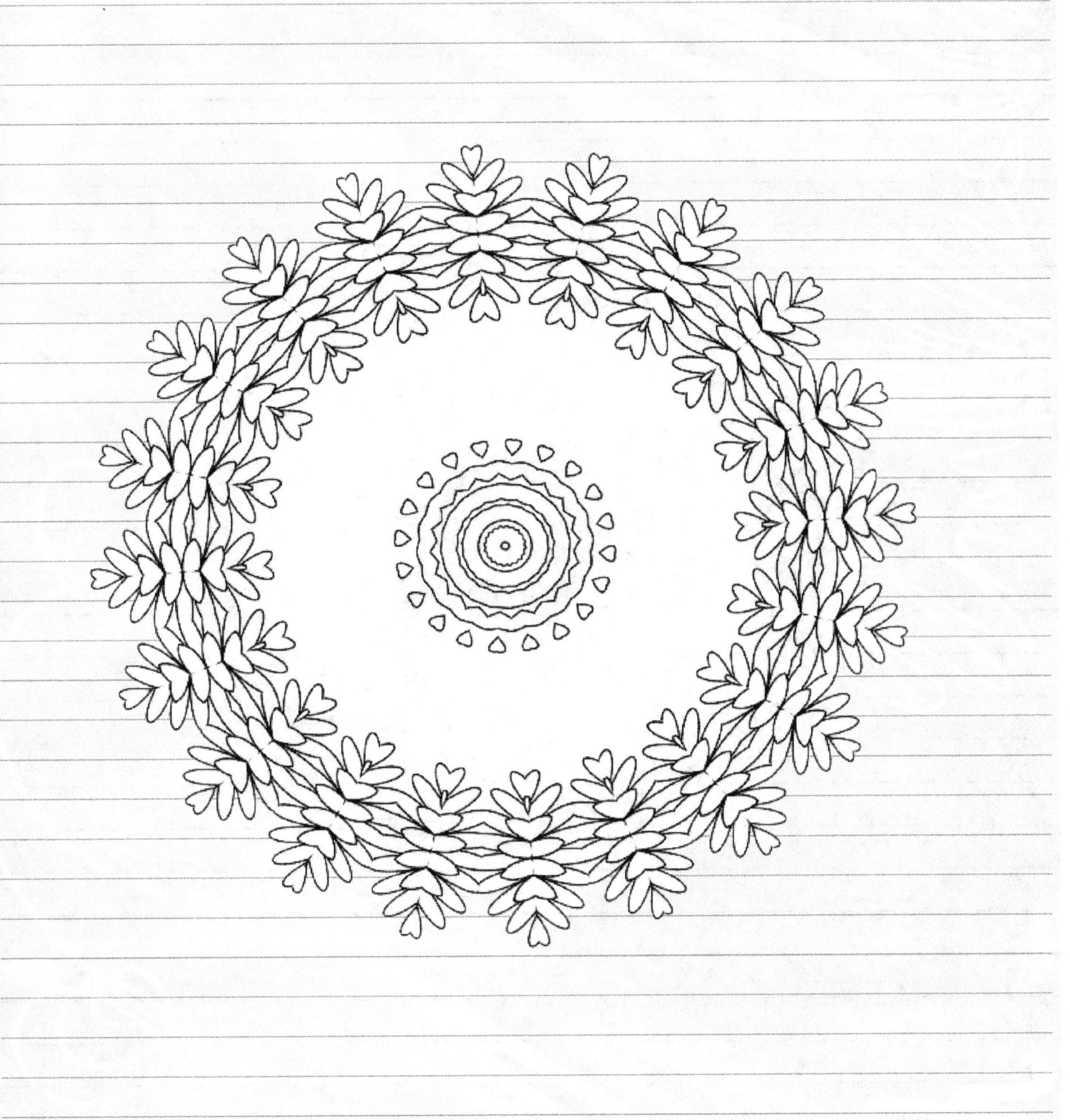

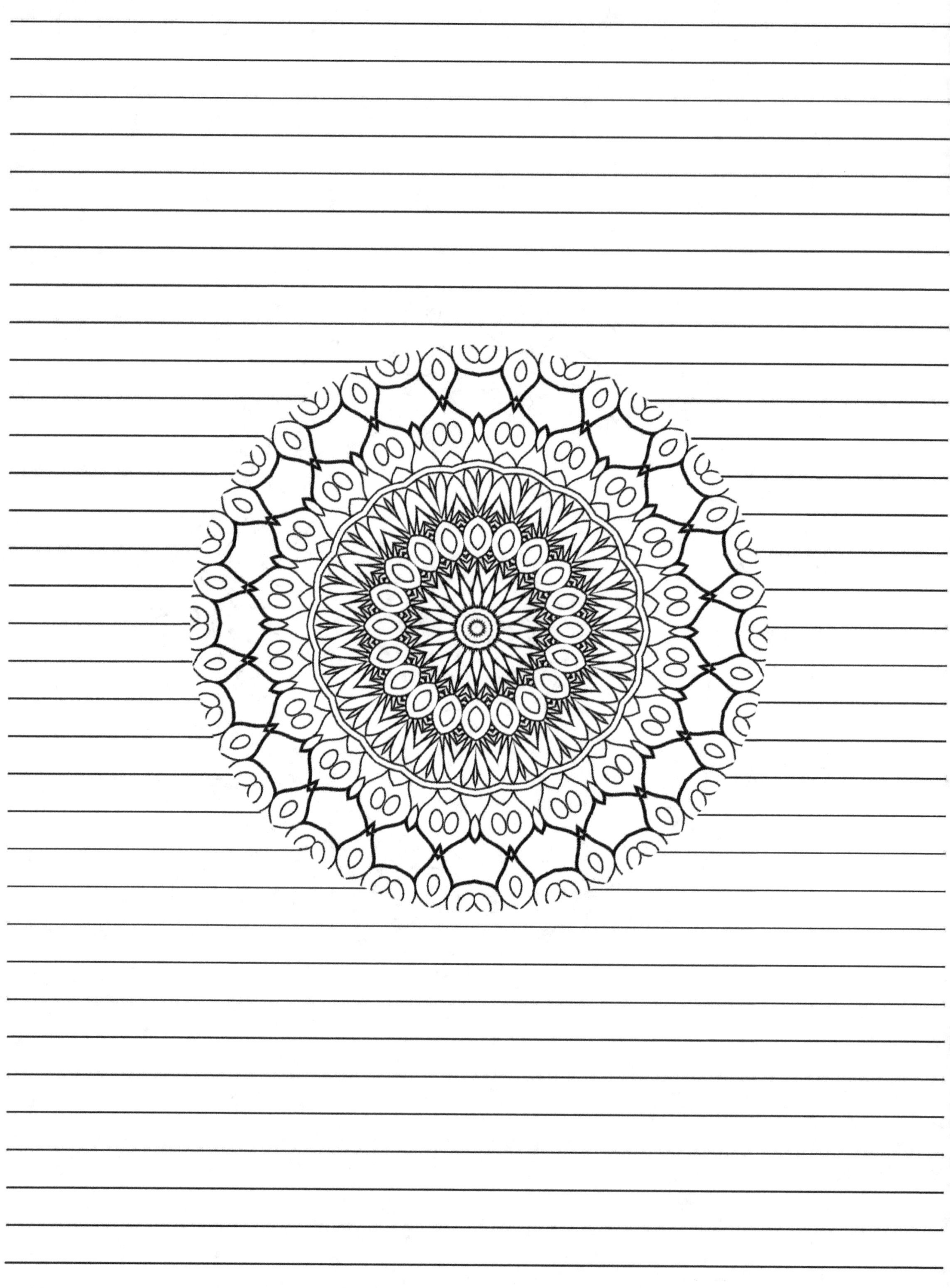

9 798710 417133